Getting Clients and Keeping Clients for Your Service Business:

A 30-Day Step-by-Step Plan

for Building Your Business

By M.D. Weems

GETTING CLIENTS AND KEEPING CLIENTS FOR YOUR SERVICE BUSINESS:
A 30-DAY STEP-BY-STEP PLAN FOR BUILDING YOUR BUSINESS
Copyright © 2008 by Atlantic Publishing Group, Inc.
1405 SW 6th Ave. • Ocala, Florida 34471 • 800-814-1132 • 352-622-1875–Fax
Web site: www.atlantic-pub.com • E-mail: sales@atlantic-pub.com
SAN Number: 268-1250

No part of this publication may be reproduced, stored in a retrieval system, or transmitted in any form or by any means, electronic, mechanical, photocopying, recording, scanning, or otherwise, except as permitted under Section 107 or 108 of the 1976 United States Copyright Act, without the prior written permission of the Publisher. Requests to the Publisher for permission should be sent to Atlantic Publishing Group, Inc., 1405 SW 6th Ave., Ocala, Florida 34471.

ISBN-13: 978-1-60138-044-9   ISBN-10: 1-60138-044-5

Library of Congress Cataloging-in-Publication Data

Weems, M. D., 1977-
  Getting clients & keeping clients for your service business : a 30-day step-by-step plan for building your business / by M.D. Weems.
     p. cm.
  Includes bibliographical references and index.
  ISBN-13: 978-1-60138-044-9 (alk. paper)
  ISBN-10: 1-60138-044-5 (alk. paper)
  1. Professions--Marketing. 2. Small business--Marketing. 3. Customer relations. I. Title.

HD8038.A1W44 2008
658.8--dc22
                         2008007341

LIMIT OF LIABILITY/DISCLAIMER OF WARRANTY: The publisher and the author make no representations or warranties with respect to the accuracy or completeness of the contents of this work and specifically disclaim all warranties, including without limitation warranties of fitness for a particular purpose. No warranty may be created or extended by sales or promotional materials. The advice and strategies contained herein may not be suitable for every situation. This work is sold with the understanding that the publisher is not engaged in rendering legal, accounting, or other professional services. If professional assistance is required, the services of a competent professional should be sought. Neither the publisher nor the author shall be liable for damages arising herefrom. The fact that an organization or Web site is referred to in this work as a citation and/or a potential source of further information does not mean that the author or the publisher endorses the information the organization or Web site may provide or recommendations it may make. Further, readers should be aware that Internet Web sites listed in this work may have changed or disappeared between when this work was written and when it is read.

INTERIOR LAYOUT DESIGN: Amber Raine • araine@atlantic-pub.com

Printed in the United States   Printed on Recycled Paper

We recently lost our beloved pet "Bear," who was not only our best and dearest friend but also the "Vice President of Sunshine" here at Atlantic Publishing. He did not receive a salary but worked tirelessly 24 hours a day to please his parents. Bear was a rescue dog that turned around and showered myself, my wife Sherri, his grandparents Jean, Bob, and Nancy and every person and animal he met (maybe not rabbits) with friendship and love. He made a lot of people smile every day.

We wanted you to know that a portion of the profits of this book will be donated to The Humane Society of the United States.

–*Douglas & Sherri Brown*

The Humane Society of the United States

The human-animal bond is as old as human history. We cherish our animal companions for their unconditional affection and acceptance. We feel a thrill when we glimpse wild creatures in their natural habitat or in our own backyard.

Unfortunately, the human-animal bond has at times been weakened. Humans have exploited some animal species to the point of extinction.

The Humane Society of the United States makes a difference in the lives of animals here at home and worldwide. The HSUS is dedicated to creating a world where our relationship with animals is guided by compassion. We seek a truly humane society in which animals are respected for their intrinsic value, and where the human-animal bond is strong.

Want to help animals? We have plenty of suggestions. Adopt a pet from a local shelter, join The Humane Society and be a part of our work to help companion animals and wildlife. You will be funding our educational, legislative, investigative, and outreach projects in the U.S. and across the globe.

Or perhaps you'd like to make a memorial donation in honor of a pet, friend, or relative? You can through our Kindred Spirits program. And if you'd like to contribute in a more structured way, our Planned Giving Office has suggestions about estate planning, annuities, and even gifts of stock that avoid capital gains taxes.

Maybe you have land that you would like to preserve as a lasting habitat for wildlife. Our Wildlife Land Trust can help you. Perhaps the land you want to share is a backyard—that's enough. Our Urban Wildlife Sanctuary Program will show you how to create a habitat for your wild neighbors.

So you see, it's easy to help animals. And The HSUS is here to help.

The Humane Society of the United States
2100 L Street NW
Washington, DC 20037
202-452-1100
www.hsus.org

Table of Contents

Introduction 11

Part One: Getting the Jump on the Competition 13

Chapter 1: Why Do People Need Your Services? 17

Chapter 2: So You Call Yourself an Expert 35

Chapter 3: "Brand" Your Business and Yourself 41

Chapter 4: Personalize It All: Logos, Brochures, and Web Sites 49

Chapter 5: Extending Your Brand to Other Areas 75

Chapter 6: Learn to Make
Your Business Visible to All.................................. 103

Chapter 7: Make Your Business
Stand Out From the Rest 107

Chapter 8: Finding Your
Target Market... 113

**Part Two: Start Your
Business's Engine 125**

Chapter 9: Create a Unique ....
Positioning Statement for Your Business 129

Chapter 10: Building Your
Business's Credibility 133

Chapter 11: Networking Is Key 137

Chapter 12: Forming Alliances
With Vendors 151

Chapter 13: Learn the Art of
the Article 155

Chapter 14: Learn to Use the
Media to Your Advantage................................ 163

Chapter 15: Some Pitfalls to Avoid 169

Part Three: Grabbing Your First Clients 177

Chapter 16: What Type of Marketing
Should You Do? 179

Chapter 17: Where Should You
Start Your Marketing? 183

Chapter 18: Marketing Success Ingredients 185

Chapter 19: Creating a Winning Plan 201

Chapter 20: Setting Goals and
Keeping Them 207

Chapter 21: Making Contacts
and Appointments 211

Chapter 22: Keeping Track of
Your Contacts 217

Chapter 23: Following Up With
Contacts After the Appointment 221

**Part Four: When Clients
Start Flooding In 227**

Chapter 24: Your First Clients 229

Chapter 25: Customer Service Basics 233

Chapter 26: Keeping Your
Employees Motivated 245

Chapter 27: The Wonder
of Referrals 249

Chapter 28: The Beauty
of Advertising 257

Chapter 29: Specials and Discounts 259

Chapter 30: Cater to Your Client Base 263

**Part Five: Keeping Your Information
Organized 267**

Chapter 31: Software to Keep
Track of It All 271

Chapter 32: Keep Your Business New 275

Conclusion: In the End 279

Bibliography 283

Biography 285

Index... 287

10 GETTING CLIENTS AND KEEPING CLIENTS FOR YOUR SERVICE BUSINESS

Introduction

Clients are the lifeblood of any business, especially a service business. Without clients, your business will not grow, and if you cannot keep the clients you have, your business will fail. Most new business owners think that when they open their doors for business, clients will simply flood in without much effort. This is not true in today's business world. With competition in every market, clients have a broad base to choose from, and they can afford to be picky and shop around. So, how do business owners gain those precious clients that they need to make their business grow and prosper?

For many business owners, finding clients can be a daunting task. At first, they try all the traditional methods — business cards and flyers, advertising in local papers, marketing promotions, and so on. But these do not always do the trick, and clients do not always respond to the traditional marketing and advertising techniques that worked ten years ago. So, business owners will turn to newer marketing and advertising venues, which can cost more money than they are really worth. Yet, they will gain clients, even if it is not at the rapid rate they had hoped. Then comes the next hard part of running a business: The business now has clients and now they must figure out how to keep them from going to their competition. This too can be a daunting task for business owners, especially if they are not customer service savvy. There are many ways a business can strive to be the best and keep the clients that they have, but sometimes these traditional ways are not enough.

This is where this book comes in. In this book are all the secrets that a business owner needs to pull in tons of clients and keep them once they come through the doors. This book will take you through all the steps that any business owner should take to ensure their client base begins to grow at a monstrous rate and to ensure they keep those clients so their business can continue to grow and prosper.

Getting Clients and Keeping Clients for Your Service Business: A 30-Day Step-by-Step Plan for Building Your Business contains all you need to know to start your business on the right track and keep it there. We have interviewed some of the best business minds out there, researched the best techniques that business owners utilize to bring in customers to their businesses, and dug into the brilliant marketing minds of the day to find the latest and best marketing strategies and information. And, we have compiled it all here, in one awesome book, to help business owners thrust their business to the next level and beyond.

Part One: Getting the Jump on the Competition

Chapter 1:   Why Do People Need Your Services?
Chapter 2:   So You Call Yourself an Expert
Chapter 3:   "Brand" Your Business and Yourself
Chapter 4:   Personalize It All: Logos, Brochures, and Web Sites
Chapter 5:   Extending Your Brand To Other Areas
Chapter 6:   Learn To Make Your Business Visible to All
Chapter 7:   Make Your Business Stand Out From the Rest
Chapter 8:   Finding Your Target Market

Day in and day out, there are new businesses that pop up all over the map. And, at the same time, there are old businesses that go out of business. This constant state of change can sometimes cause a sense of confusion in clients who like certain aspects of a business that just shut down, and do not care much for those that have just started up. But, with all the different service businesses out there, they can easily change if they do not like the first one that they choose.

Face it, the simple reality of business is that there is always another business there to take your place if you fail. By keeping this in mind, you need to gain the upper hand over your competition when it comes to pulling in new clients. Getting the jump on your competition will help to ensure you will not only gain new clients, but keep them over time, since you are able to offer them something that the others cannot. But there are several steps that you need to take to ensure you have the jump on the competition. These beginning steps will help to establish you and your business as experts in your area, gain a recognizable "brand" that clients will instantly associate with you, and make your business jump out above the competition so that clients will know you are the best around. By implementing these simple steps, you can rest assured that your business will have the upper hand.

Any smart business owner knows instinctively that they need to make their business stand out from the rest. But most business owners do not know how to do this the right way. There are hundreds of thousands of ways that you can push your business, but not all of these ways will bring clients into your business, and most can push them in the opposite direction.

To begin to build your business so that clients will want to use you and stay with you, you need to develop a firm foundation for both you and your business to stand on. This means you need to establish yourself as an expert in your area, and you need to be a credible pillar in your business area as well. You will also need to establish a credible and trustworthy image for your business that will show clients that you are a professional and your business is here to stay and to serve them as long as they need you. By creating a platform that you can build your business and your reputation upon, you will create a sturdy foundation that you can continue to build from for many years to come.

The first part of this book will help you take the steps needed to build the firm foundation that any good business owner and service business needs to continue to grow and prosper in today's competitive market. So, make sure you read through and understand this area of building your business on a rock-solid foundation so you are prepared to head on to the next part of this book.

Chapter 1: Why Do People Need Your Services?

In this chapter, you will learn why people need your services and how to show them that they need your services. There are several steps that go into determining why clients need your services, which is one of the building blocks for a strong foundation for your business. Here are the steps that we will go over in this chapter:

- Learning to identify your target clients and your target markets

- Learning to identify the wants and needs of those clients and markets

- Learning to offer great opportunities for investments to those clients and markets

- Learning the best ways to find and show the benefits that clients will gain from your opportunity

Learning to Identify Your Target Clients and Your Target Markets

The first step you will need to take in identifying your target clients and markets is to determine which clients you want to work with. Why should you worry about which clients you want to work with — after all, are not all clients good to work with? Not exactly. When you determine which type of clients you love to work with, you will then be doing work that you love to do. In turn, this will ensure every second of your work will be the best work that you do and is one of the main ways your clients will gain respect and trust in you and your business.

When you are able to pick out your ideal clients, no matter if they are individuals or other businesses, you will be placing yourself with clients who actually inspire you to do your best. Remember when you were a teenager and you had one friend who your parents thought was a bad influence on you? They constantly told you that one person was a "bad influence" on you, and that one person would ruin your reputation, right? Yet, another friend was a "good influence" on you, and made your reputation better. You probably even heard, "You are the company you keep" once or twice from them too.

The same is true in business, yet most business owners overlook this extremely important aspect.

Most business owners simply take any client with a checkbook that comes through their door. But, if these businesses took the time to work with the clients who are ideal for them, they would find that all the clients who cause undo stress and frustration will disappear. Only those clients who truly inspire a business owner to produce the best possible work will remain.

By identifying your target clients, and those clients who do not fit into your plan, you will be creating a special area that only caters to those clients who will help your business grow and help you grow as a business owner. Think of this step as creating a VIP area for your clients. This VIP area, or your business, is only for certain clients, those that you choose to work with. But, to truly create a great VIP area, you will need to get rid of those clients who are less than VIP status.

Sorting Out the VIP Clients

There are several authors who also preach this same theory. If business owners would simply sort out their non-VIP clients, they would have the best ones left to work with. In *Book Yourself Solid: The Fastest, Easiest, and Most Reliable System for Getting More Clients Than You Can Handle Even if You Hate Marketing and Selling*, Michael Port tells us to "dump the duds," or dump those clients who do not fit into your VIP area.

I know you are wondering why you would dump clients when this book is supposed to help you gain them and keep them, right? Well, this does not mean you need to get rid of all your clients, only the ones who seem to drain you or those who treat you and your business with a less than desirable attitude. Ask yourself which clients on your list seem to completely drain the energy out of you and end up leaving you feeling less than whole after a visit. Make a list of the clients who you simply dread dealing with and why you do not care to deal with them.

This next part may be hard for you, as it usually is for most business owners. You need to start the process of weeding out those non-VIP clients from your business. Your first step in creating your VIP area is to make a list of characteristics or behaviors that you prefer and a list of those that you do not want to deal with in your business. Keep in mind that you will have to be completely honest with yourself and honest about your clients, even if they are your friends. If you are not honest, then this will not work, and your newly found VIP status will not work for your benefit.

Now, look through this list and place your current clients on one side or the other. If you are having trouble in choosing where certain clients should go, place them on a "maybe" list. Your VIP clients should be those whom you absolutely love to deal with, those who inspire you to learn the newest techniques, or those who make you feel that your business is worthwhile. Your non-VIP clients should be those who completely drain the life out of you when you have to deal with them, those who are less than desirable to work with, and those who make you cringe each time you hear their names.

Here comes the part that will be the hardest for most money-minded business owners — those clients who were placed on your non-VIP list are those who need to be cut from your client list. Do not panic — I know the thought of actually cutting clients from your list is not what you want to hear at the beginning of this book. You are probably feeling a bit sick at the thought of losing clients — paying clients — but it is all right.

Keep in mind that to create a solid foundation for your business, you will need to replace those pillars that do not help hold up the weight of the business. This means cutting the clients that are on your non-VIP list.

You should also remember that cutting those non-VIP clients is just as much for their good as it is for yours. The clients who completely drain you, or force you to cringe at the thought of their names, are obviously not getting the best services from you. You owe it to them to cut them and refer them to another service provider who can take better care of them.

Also, remember that you are your clients. Who would you rather have your business associated with — clients who love your business and rave about how great you are, or clients who are not completely satisfied or who are never satisfied with anything and are more likely to give you a bad referral to other clients? The more VIP clients you have, the better your reputation will become, and the more referrals you will get from the clients' friends and family who have heard them rave about how great you are and how wonderful your services are.

When you work with clients who do not fit into your VIP list, there will come a point when conflict will arise between you and the client, intentional or not. Both you and the client will become frustrated with the business arrangement, and the client will think they are not getting the best service from you. They will be right too, since you will not be giving your best to them since you do not like to deal with that particular client. So, it does not benefit either one of you for you to keep them on as a client. If you keep them on because you are afraid to cut them from your VIP list, then you will end up with former clients who go out into the world and tell everyone what a terrible service provider you are.

While not all clients will be the right fit for your VIP list, they will fit onto someone else's list. There is nothing wrong with the client, no matter what you may feel; they are just not right for your VIP list. So, you are not "firing" them; you simply need to find them another service provider that fits them better.

When you are ready to find those non-VIP clients a new service provider, be sure you choose your words carefully. It is easy to say what you feel, but if you choose your words carefully and truly convey that you are trying to get them the best service possible, you will come across as a truthful, diplomatic person, and not a jerk. Do not worry about coming up with a long explanation. Keep it simple and the client will appreciate that. You can say something like: "I am not the right person to service your needs," or "I do not think that we are a good fit, but I know a few other service providers who would be perfect for you."

Of course, not all of your non-VIP clients are going to like this. You will not always get a loving response with a big hug at the end. More than likely, you will get a bad response, so you cannot be too thin-skinned. Remember that you cannot please everyone all the time. So, as long as you are diplomatic, tactful, and respectful, you will be able to keep your dignity, and your client's, intact.

When you look over the benefits of working with VIP clients who fit you and your business well, you should get a great feeling inside that you are moving your business in the right direction. To begin your VIP list, start with this exercise: Make a list of the benefits that you feel you get from working with your ideal VIP clients. Here are some points that may grace your list:

- They inspire you to do your best work.

- They make you feel like a success.

- They boost your confidence.

- They let you know your work matters to others.

- They give you extra energy to help make you a better business owner.

- They help make you feel invigorated.

- They connect with you on a deeper level than other clients.

Of course, there will be other points on your list that will be specific to your service area, and feel free to make as long, or short, a list as you need.

Next, make a list of the qualities that your ideal VIP clients will possess. Here are some points that may grace this list for you:

- They naturally bond with you and your business.
- They seem to focus easily on what you are telling them.
- They are smart.
- They are loyal to your business and you.
- They are polite.
- They value your services.
- They are positive.

Just like your previous list, there will be other points that will be specific to your service area and to your personal values that will help to shape your VIP wish list.

The lists that you create will look different and will probably be a lot longer. These are just samples to show you what you need to place on each list. Make sure you are placing as many factors on your list as you need to ensure you cover all the bases for what makes a great client for you and your business.

Now, take your lists and look at your current clients. Find your top five to ten favorite clients who seem to encompass all of these aspects that make up your VIP wish lists. Write down the top five reasons that you like working with these clients, and be honest with this list. Compare this list to your other lists and see which points are on all three of your lists. When you find points that are similar, then you will know that is one of the main qualities you value in your best clients.

With these lists, you can now begin to narrow down your parameters in selecting clients for your business. Combine your lists, with the top five points from each one, all on a master list. This will become your client filter and will help you to choose only those clients who fit onto your VIP list. You can now use these filters to go through your client base and select those clients that meet at least 75 percent of those filters. Once you have these filters in place, you will automatically begin to sort out those non-VIP clients and gain only the ones that will fit into your VIP status.

These VIP clients who fit into your business filters are your target clients and target markets. The next step is to learn how to identify the wants and needs of the VIP clients that fall into your target market.

Learning to Identify the Wants and Needs of Clients and Markets

Now that you have learned how to weed out the non-VIP clients and create a target client and target market list, you are ready to learn how to identify the wants and needs of those VIP clients that you want to gain for your business. The main goal of identifying your target clients and markets is to allow your business to better determine where to find those clients who want or need what your business offers. Once you are able to determine where to find these clients, you can concentrate your marketing and advertising to that specific area, instead of the whole market.

Keep in mind that marketing and sales are not used to try to manipulate or convince people into purchasing your services. A good marketing and sales campaign is about getting your business in front of those people who already need your services and offering them something that they cannot currently find with other service providers. You have a specific target market that you are meant to serve, but you cannot serve them until you know where to find them. This is why it is important to know exactly what your target market is.

This part of Chapter 1 will also teach you to go against popular belief when it comes to marketing and advertising. You need to learn to narrow your marketing to a specific group of people, your target market, instead of marketing to everyone at the same time. It is a common belief in marketing that the more people you are able to market to, the more clients you will get. This is not true. Remember that you cannot please everyone all the time, and there is no need to try. If you could do everything for every client, then you would eventually lose business because some clients would fall by the wayside. So, trying to be everything to everyone is just impossible. But, if you can be everything to that specific target market where your VIP clients are, then you have found your target market and you will find that your business will grow faster than you can imagine.

So, here is where the hard part comes in. You need to begin to change your marketing thinking and begin to narrow your marketing campaigns down to fit into your target market. For example, if you offer services that mainly benefit seniors, you do not want to run a marketing campaign that will target teenagers and younger adults also. Your marketing campaign will get a better response by targeting VIP clients in the senior section, and will bring in more potential clients.

You can probably think of a thousand reasons why you cannot narrow down your market and begin to specialize your services to one area. But take a look at any specialist in any area. Those are the providers who are always booked solid because they are experts in their fields and they specialize in one area, not several. By specializing in one area of your industry, you will be able to offer the best possible service to clients who need that particular service and you will be enjoying what you do, not dreading it.

Finding Your Target Client Base and Target Market

If you are having trouble trying to figure out what your target market is, or what your specialties are, then here is your chance to do it. This part of the chapter will help you find those certain items in your service business that you are passionate about, those areas that prove you have a natural talent for them, and make you stand out above the competition.

First, consider what you truly love the most about your business. Which service do you provide that almost feels more like getting paid to play than working? Which service do you provide that is your absolute favorite to perform? Which service do you provide that proves you have a wonderful natural talent for this service?

This part is all about you. You can be a little selfish here, because if you are able to identify those specific areas that you are always psyched up about, you will be able to more easily identify your target market. If you are not excited about what you do, then it is not your target market. For example, if you are a psychologist and you see everyone from children to seniors, but you absolutely love to work with children under ten, then this is your target market. You should begin to narrow down your services to children under ten since this is the area that you love and that area that will allow you to excel in your industry.

Here is the tricky part to narrowing down your service business: narrow it down to a specific area that you truly love. Do not simply choose the area that you feel will make the most money, or that you feel is in the highest demand. By choosing an area based on money or demand, it will not take long for you to become bored and disheartened with what you have chosen and you will be right back in the same rut that you started from. You need to choose the area that makes you happy, an area that you are passionate about. When you are doing something that you love, then your business will succeed because you will be putting out your best work. You should have a gut feeling about which area of your service profession you should be focusing on; an internal pull toward one area or another. Listen to this feeling, as it is usually right on target with what your love truly is.

Of course, you should also consider your clients when you are making your decision. Look at the common elements in your clients, such as age, profession, location, industry, and so on. When you are ready to look at narrowing down your service business, here is what you need to do:

Write down a list of the different groups of clients that use your services. This can be groups such as seniors, business professionals, travelers, teenagers, restaurant owners, and so on. Then take a look at this list and put a mark by the groups that you love to work with and that inspire you to be the best you can and offer the best services for them. Now, which of these groups on your list do you already have clients in? Which groups do you have the most experience with or which ones do you find the most interesting? And finally, where are your natural talents in your area?

Take a look at your answers to these questions and your list of groups that you already cater to. Do you see any similarities? Chances are, you will. You should look at which groups you truly love to work with, and begin to look at how you can use your natural talents and passions to help those groups in your work. And, listen to your gut. If it tells you that you should be heading into one area, that is probably the best fit for you.

Learn to Identify the Wants and Needs of Your Target Market

It is the wants and needs of clients that drives them to seek the services you provide. Therefore, you need to offer what your potential clients want or need to purchase, not simply what you prefer to sell to them or what you think that they should be purchasing from you. Take a good, long look at your business and services as if you were the client who needed them. Put yourself in their shoes and see what it is that you would want or need if you were them; you will find that it is not just what you like to sell.

The wants and needs of clients is what pushes them to find you in the first place and what binds them to you when they continue to want or need your services. Take the time to truly think about the wants and needs of your clients. For example, why did you purchase this book? Is it because you just wanted to buy a book? No, it is because you wanted or needed the information inside.

You want to gain more clients and you need to make your business more successful, right? This same thing is true with your clients.

Once you can identify their wants and needs, you can easily tailor your services to meet them and start to see more clients come through your doors. You will also be able to better show them the return on their investment in you and your business if you completely understand their wants and needs, which is our next step.

Learning to Offer Great Opportunities for Investments to Those Clients and Markets

Ask yourself this: do your clients see your business or services as an opportunity that will give them a good return on their investment with you? Any potential client should be able to see your services as an investable opportunity, one in which they feel they will see a return that is greater than the money, or investment, that they spent.

Of course, this return on their investment in you will come in many different forms, depending on what services you offer them. But, keep in mind that your clients will want to receive an emotional and even a financial return on their investment in you, which they will want to see before they sign that check. A financial return? Yes, that is right. While it may not be in the form of a monetary gain later on, there are several different forms of financial returns that your clients can see. For example, a monetary return would be a client attending a seminar that teaches them how to sell real estate. They invested $50 for the tickets and information for the seminar, but they took the information they learned and made $25,000 on their first sale. This is a great monetary return. A different type of monetary return would be a medical professional helping a client. The client pays their co-pay or insurance, and the medical professional helps to cure them or make them feel better. This, in turn, allows the client to continue their job and their normal lifestyle, which allows them a better financial return than if they were still sick or hurt and could not work or enjoy their normal life. There are thousands of examples for each different service industry that can illustrate how each client can gain a monetary and emotional return from your services.

One of the main secrets to finding that successful niche for your business is to understand and know what your clients want and need from you. So, instead of simply talking to your clients about your services, help them to see a clear picture of what you can do to help satisfy their wants and needs. By showing them up front that the initial investment that they are making in you is worth it in the long run, you will gain more clients and be able to provide exactly the services that they are looking for.

Once your clients understand exactly what you can do for them to help satisfy their wants and needs, they will make every effort that they possibly can to work with you. You can then move on to the next step of the process, which is to find the best ways to showcase the benefits that your clients will gain from your services.

Learning the Best Ways to Find and Show the Benefits That Clients Will Gain From Your Opportunity

To make your investment and return opportunity completely clear to your clients, you need to be able to understand and demonstrate the benefits that you can offer them. The opportunities that you can offer — which is the service that you provide, such as counseling, financial services, Web design, writing, and so on — are simply the things that you do in your business. These are the tangible services that you offer to clients, which are technically what your clients are buying from you, but not actually what they are really buying from you.

How does that make sense? Well, let us look at the opportunities that you purchased when you bought this book:

- The opportunity to learn what you need to do to make your business grow

- The opportunity to see what you can do to expand your client base to the limits

- The opportunity for access to this training program that will teach you all you need to know in 30 days

But these are only the features that you purchased when you bought this book. The actual benefits that you are purchasing are deeper than just those simple things. While some of the benefits are tangible and you will be able to actually see and touch the results, there are other benefits that you will not be able to see or touch that are just as important.

Let us look at the real reason you purchased this book. Ask yourself why you bought it. Would you say that you want to gain more clients? Or how about that you want more money in your bank account and your wallet?

Well, while these things may be those tangible items that you can see and touch, there are other things that you gain as well. The truth is: You are not really after more clients or more money. Stick with me here, I know that sounds odd. What you are really after is the peace of mind that comes along with owning a successful business. You want the financial freedom that other successful business owners enjoy, and the time that you will then gain with your family, friends, or just doing what you love to do on your personal time. Does this sound like the real reasons that you started up your service business? Are not these the real reasons that you purchased this book too?

Now that you know the real reasons that you purchased this book, it will be easier for you to identify why your clients really need or want your services. And, the more benefits that you can unearth and the more reasons why your clients need your services, the better you will become at providing them with what they need.

Here is a great exercise that you can do at any time to help you see what the real reasons are that your clients are coming to you: Write down all of the deeper benefits that your clients will get from your services. Write down as many as you possibly can, even if they are a bit far-fetched, and see how long you can make your list. Then read back over them once a week or more to remind yourself why you are providing this service.

Your Clients Want You to Help Them

Once you understand that every client you have wants your help, you will become more successful in your business. Your clients view you as an advisor — someone they trust and whose opinions they value. They need you to counsel them, advise them, hold their hand, and guide them through their problem until they can see the solution at the other end.

They need you to be their leader. Once you start to see yourself as a leader for your clients, you will be able to fill that role and give your clients someone to believe in. Once they believe in you and see you as a leader instead of a "yes man," they will continue to come back to you next month, next year, and beyond. You cannot expect this to happen immediately, because trust is something that happens over a period of time. But, if you can begin to show that you are a leader and trustworthy, your clients will start to gain trust in you and they will speak about that trust to other clients and potential clients.

Once you completely understand why your clients want and need to purchase your services by learning the four key points of this chapter, you will start to notice changes in your business, in your clients, and in yourself. Once these changes take place, you can begin to move on to the next step in our book: being an expert in your field.

Chapter 2: So You Call Yourself an Expert

Expert. Just that one little word can add so much credibility to you and your business. You hear it all the time, "Dr. So-and-So is an expert in child care," or "Mrs. So-and-So is an expert designer." Experts are everywhere, and those who can say they are experts gain more respect, more clients, and more business than you can imagine. One of the first steps in developing your "brand" is to be able to use your expertise in your service industry to gain the respect and trust of your clients and peers.

By branding the business knowledge that you have gained around your business, you can begin to use your knowledge to exert confidence, competence, and leadership in a way that your target markets and target clients will find appealing to their needs and wants. When you are able to achieve an expert status, you instantly transform yourself from simply another business owner to a trusted leader that has a vast wealth of knowledge about your chosen industry. You will no longer be another business owner who is advertising and marketing for their chunk of the pie. You will rise up onto a higher platform that will enable you to reach out to more clients that fit into your VIP area and enable you the time and the money to weed out those that fit more on your non-VIP list.

It was not that long ago that the word "expert" was synonymous with how many college hours you had, how many years in the business you had, or how many classes or seminars you had taught. In recent years, this thinking has changed. As more people become interested in their business results, they have found that the word "expert" has nothing to do with the amount of college credits you have or the length of time you have been in business. It all revolves around your personal knowledge and your love for the field that you are in.

Experts are always sought after, no matter which field they are in. Experts gain more business with less marketing, advertising, and effort. Experts are interviewed by journalists and others who need information on a specific area. Experts are asked to teach classes and seminars and speak at conferences. Experts place themselves way above the rest of the pack and are recognized for it.

Learn to Be an Expert in Your Field

No one can tell you that you can, or cannot, be successful. On the same hand, no one can tell you that you can, or cannot, become an expert. You do not have to take a ton of tests, go through thousands of college hours, or write thousands of books on a subject to be an expert either. You do not have to be appointed or elected as an expert in your field. You can do it all yourself.

While becoming an expert does take a lot of work, it is within your reach. Once you have narrowed down your business to the services that you truly love to provide and do, then you are able to focus on those specific areas and become an expert in them. You simply need to be willing to learn everything possible and continue to learn to be able to classify yourself as an expert.

I am not saying that you have to learn all there is to know about your field before you can say you are an expert. I am simply saying you need to be willing to learn, and continue to learn, all you can about your specialty. Once you are able to commit to learning all you can about your chosen field, then you will be able to develop a strategy that will help you understand all the information you possibly can about your target market. Remember that you do not need to know everything, because that is impossible, but you will need to learn enough that you are more knowledgeable than your peers and others in your field. You should also keep in mind that keeping yourself in the expert position is a constant process and you will always be learning new techniques, styles, and other areas of your field to keep in front of the crowd.

The future of your business and your status as an expert all depend on how you develop yourself. You can create the best possible brochures, advertising campaigns, marketing packages, and so on, but if you do not continue your education, you will not remain in the highly competitive spot that you have worked so hard to place yourself into. Make sure you are constantly examining yourself for gaps in your knowledge so you can continue to fill them. An expert in any field knows that the field is constantly changing and he or she must change as well to keep up with it.

Create a Unique Viewpoint

Now that you know you will constantly be learning to be able to continue to be called an expert, you need to work on creating a unique viewpoint that will distinguish you from other experts and professionals in your field. This is when you set your strategy and expertise into your branding strategy so you can create a personalized viewpoint that no one else has. Learn what others in your field are saying about, writing about, and doing in your industry. This goes along with your quest to continue learning all you can about your field, but also goes a long way in helping to establish your specific stance. By knowing all the other viewpoints out there, you can establish a perspective that will make a connection between you and your business and the others in your field throughout the world.

Immerse yourself in current discussions that are going on in your field right now. You can find these online in chat rooms, forums, publications, newsletters, and even at trade events. Make it your goal to put yourself into as many discussions as possible so you can start to form your viewpoint and express it.

All experts know they have to seek out all new evidence and new information about their fields so they can constantly change, or solidify, their viewpoints and theories. They are always on the prowl for case studies, research, new information, statistics, and more that can help to substantiate or change their thinking and viewpoint.

Keep in mind that you do not have to create an "ultimate truth," but you do need to be able to state your position clearly and state the facts that you have found that support that theory.

Read, Read, Read

When you were in grade school, your teachers and parents probably preached the importance of reading. Well, the same is still true in the business world, especially when you are establishing and keeping up with your expert status. Search for the most up-to-date information available for your field, both online and off. You can subscribe to newsletters, magazines, news services, forums, chat rooms, Web sites, and all sorts of media that can help bring you the most information possible. The good thing is, with the wealth of knowledge available on the Internet today, you no longer have to spend thousands of dollars a year on print publications if you do not want to. You can simply place yourself on some of the better newsletter mailing lists and subscribe to some of the best Web sites that bring the information that you need.

But, when you are reading these publications, do not just focus on the contents of the articles. Study the whole thing, the words, the lingo, the points, and the person who wrote it. Most writers specialize in one particular industry such as medical, technology, or finance, and you will begin to see their names over and over as you read more and more information. Keep track of the writers who seem to have the same point of view as you, or who make the same arguments that you do for a particular cause. Make note of them and keep their names familiar to you, as they can become great messengers for your business.

Find a great bookstore in town and start to become a regular there. Make sure the bookstore you choose has a great selection of books that deal with your industry, so you will know where you can turn to purchase the latest editions of books that can help you in your practice. This way, you will always know where you can turn for an immediate and dependable information boost.

When you read up on the latest information in your field on a regular basis, you will always be sure to have the latest information to help keep your expert status intact.

Showcase Yourself as a Reliable Resource

Once you have your fingers on the pulse of the latest information for your field and you begin to develop your personal viewpoints and opinions, you can then start to work on the task of becoming a resource yourself. Start to give away free information to clients, business owners, and anyone who needs the information. This information can come in many forms — booklets, reports, Web content, articles, white papers, press releases, brochures, and so on. There are literally thousands of different forms that you can use to give away information. The more information you have available to clients and others, the more they will start to see you as an expert in that area. You will then become their "go-to" person for new information and any questions or concerns they may have. And, when people already like to do business with you, you will automatically become their first choice for information about your field.

Remember that the center of influence is always a visible source for the latest information. So you need to be sure you are visible to your clients, business partners, others in your field, and the public in general. Make sure you are constantly coming up with strategies that will have your name, face, and information out in front of people, no matter if it is in the form of written, spoken, or visual information.

Also, when you become a center of influence for your field, you need to be sure that you "walk the walk" while you "talk the talk." Your credibility will go through the roof if you show the world that you are completely confident in the messages you espouse.

Now that you have established yourself as an expert in your area, you can start to develop your own personal brand, and brand your business.

Chapter 3
"Brand" Your Business and Yourself

So you have now learned exactly why people need your services, how to narrow down your business to do what you truly love to do, created a filter to gain you only the VIP clients that you want to work with, and you have established yourself as an expert in your field. Sounds like a lot, does it not? Well, that is just the beginning. Your next step in gaining more clients is to "brand" your business and yourself.

A personal brand is like stepping out above the competition. You create a personal brand to serve you and your business as your key to success. Your personal brand will be able to clearly identify both you and your business, as it will define your business and you, express what you stand for, and communicate everything about you and your business to the world. By conveying exactly who you are and what you stand for, you will start to pull in those VIP clients with this personal brand before they ever hear an advertisement or marketing promotion from you. Your personal brand will also push away those non-VIP clients who you worked so hard to filter out of your service business.

However, a personal brand is much more than what you do. A personal brand is you. Your personal brand will be unique and will allow you to distinguish yourself from all the others in your field and will showcase who you are and what you stand for to everyone.

If you look at the retail sales market today, you can find so many brand names that are synonymous for certain products that have many different brands. For example, take the "Palm Pilot." Even though the Palm company had to change the name of their famous personal assistant, the name stuck and most people today still use this term to describe their new PDA. Since brand names are used to distinguish products and services from each other, just about every business is looking for a way to make their product or service completely unique from all the others.

Branding is no longer just for tangible products. Branding is for services and other businesses as well. And by branding a business no longer linked to only products, businesses all over the world can begin to brand their names and services so they are more easily recognizable. There are several different functions that a brand can allow you and your business the freedom to do:

- The ability to build an extremely strong client and customer loyalty.

- The ability to bring more credibility to any project.

- The ability to deliver any message fast and effectively.

- The ability to hit an emotional level with people.

- The ability to separate yourself and your business from the competition.

- The ability to position a focused message in both the heart and mind of your target market.

- The ability to be consistent in your marketing promotions and campaigns.

When you are a small business owner, it may seem that "branding" your business or yourself can simply be a "slick" advertising movement. But branding your small business is more about putting your business and yourself in front of your target market so that they can see your business as the best choice above the others. When you build a business brand, it is not only about what you do, it is also about what makes you different from the other choices out there.

In the book *The Revenge of Brand X*, author Rob Frankel says, "Branding is about getting prospects to see you as the only solution to their problems." He points out that a business wants their target market to see the competition that is out there, and then book it straight to you since they see you as the only solution. It is this type of thinking that will not only get them in your door, but will keep them coming back again and again.

Your Brand Is Your Soul

Once you create your business's "brand," it becomes the life and soul of your company. It will hold together your entire marketing and advertising strategies and will help to connect your business to your clients and your market. The brand you create will convey your business's personality, abilities, and aura that surround your business. You want this brand to be a bit mysterious, but at the same time to convey what you stand for and what you are.

Many businesses out there have developed brands. And it is easy to see which brands do their job, and which do not. An effective brand will send a complete message that will encompass the whole business, and will include a special logo that will be everywhere in the business: on stationery, cards, packaging, signs, and more. This brand also will fit right in the pricing of the services or products, customer services, and the business's guarantees.

When you think of a "brand," you normally see a slogan, logo, or other stand-out item from a certain business that you are familiar with. But a true brand is more than just this simple thing. In the book *Be Your Own Brand*, authors Karl Speak and David McNally write: "When most people think of a brand, they visualize a slogan, a logo, a campaign, a promise, or a product. A brand is much more." They continue with, "Your company's brand is a powerful relationship fueled by a loyal belief system and knotted to the principle of providing exceptional value."

No matter if your brand is positive, negative, or in the middle, each company has a brand. This brand will help to describe the complete experience that comes with doing business with you, which includes using your services or products. So, when you are considering if your brand is right for you or not, check your brand against these questions:

1. Does your brand express market relevance to your potential clients and existing ones?

2. Does your brand stand for something that is meaningful to your clients and target market?

3. Does your brand stand up to the promise that your clients or customers will have the same experience with your business every time?

4. Does your brand help clients or customers to feel confident in your business so they continue to return for your help?

5. Does your brand promote a strong relationship between you, your business, and your clients?

6. Does your brand exude a strong bond so that clients and customers refer their family and friends to you?

7. Does your brand promote loyalty in your clients and customers?

8. Does your brand help to promote a good reputation with both potential and existing customers?

A good brand will have you answering "yes" to all of these questions. If you find you have answered "no," or you are not sure about your brand, then it may be time to reexamine your brand and see if a change is needed in your brand or your business.

Branding Your Business's Personality

"Personality branding" is a unique strategy that promotes both you and your business's personality and helps to incorporate it into your brand so that it will create an emotional bond between you and your market. This helps to put a "human face" on your business and your brand by promoting your unique personality and making it one of the main pillars of your business. Personality branding is also a great way to help express your passion and your business's passion to the whole world, including any potential clients who are still on the fence about your business. When you can put a person behind your business, it will add an extra air of humanity to your business and will put a human face on your business so that it is not just another large corporation.

Your Brand Is Your Promise

In today's highly competitive business world, brand marketing is becoming more important than ever. Your business's brand should be its defense against the entire world. This brand is your promise to everyone. Busy clients do not have the time to examine all the choices when they need to make a decision. They have to be able to believe in a brand since they have already heard everything, seen everything, and have been scammed by outrageous claims and nonsense by other businesses. So, before they spend their hard-earned money with you, they need to be sure you will stand up behind your promise.

Since today's consumers have already had bad experiences and have so many different choices when it comes to businesses, just being good at what you do is no longer enough. You must start to build your brand so you can always deliver on your promises and provide customer satisfaction each time a consumer purchases from you. Your brand should promise value to your customers, it should promise the best possible experience, and it should promise the best possible service to each person. Your brand should give people something to trust in that will also help them to identify with your business and services in this crazy business world. Your brand should show your customers you know what they want and need, and you can provide it for them anytime, anywhere.

Ten Steps to Creating a Winning Brand

But where do you start when you want to create a winning brand that will help customers identify your business with everything that will make them feel completely comfortable and confident with you? Here are ten steps that you should follow when you are creating your own brand:

1. **Values** — To start your brand on the right track, you should know what your personal and business values are.

Make a list of both personal and business values and then create a value statement for your business that is based on this list that is 25 words or less.

2. **Mission** — You should also start with your business values by creating a mission statement. A good mission statement is meaningful, but still short enough to remember by everyone.

3. **Vision** — Your next step is to create a vision statement. A good vision statement will answer this question: "How will you know when you have done what you said you would do in your mission statement?" Every business should have a vision, and continually strive to meet it.

4. **Starting Point** — Look at where you and your business stand right now when it comes to your vision. Write down a simple statement that tells you where you and your business are on the road to your ultimate vision.

5. **Market** — This is where you need to know your target market. Use the previous exercises that you did in this book to list your target market.

6. **Positioning** — Create a positioning statement that will help to sort out the "mental" real estate that your business is striving to own. This should also encompass how you want your target market to see your business.

7. **Name** — Now, name your business so that it captures everything that your business does. This is the most important step in this whole process. A good name is not generic, and a generic name will only breed generic business.

The name should incorporate your personality, mission, vision, and everything that makes your vision unique.

8. **Logo** — When you establish your logo, you should make sure it will strike a cord with your market. It should create a unique thought in your clients' minds, which will immediately identify your business to them. It should be a positive logo that promotes a positive image of your business and helps to represent the promise that you make to your customers.

9. **Microbrand** — By microbranding your business, you create a new world of business opportunities. Once you see the powerful network you already have in place, you can then use it to define your brand farther and help your business grow. Start by listing all the contacts and influential people that you know, and then make a list of all the important events that you need to start attending to help you build this list.

10. **Spread the Word** — Those businesses that are successful microbranders are able to get other people and business owners talking about them. Find out who the most influential people are in your specific industry and see if you already know them. If not, determine what you need to do to meet them. By knowing the most powerful people in your industry, you open the door to place your business in front of power people.

Once you have your brand firmly in place, you need to move on to our next step of developing a logo, brochures, and many other aspects of sales and marketing where your brand will make you stand out from the others in your field.

Chapter 4
Personalize It All: Logos, Brochures, and Web Sites

With all the new ways that a business can use the Internet to gain contacts and clients, there is an unlimited source of business to be found. When you are able to tap into this business, then you can see your business soar. Now that you have defined your target market by narrowing down your business, started to establish yourself as an expert in your area, and have started to brand your business, your next step is to personalize everything for your business. When you personalize your business information and tools, your clients and potential clients start to see your business as a professional one that will be around for a long time.

These tools are the bread and butter of your business, and you cannot do without them. By placing your brand on all of your sales and business tools, you will be able to take your new brand from a simple idea to a marketing force to be reckoned with.

Logo Time

A logo is a single symbol that helps people recognize your personal brand. A good logo can tell people just about everything that they need to know about your business: your name, what you do, your business style, value, and more. This logo will be placed everywhere, from your business cards to brochures, and Web sites to marketing campaigns, so you need to be able to create a great personal logo for your business that will be the heart and soul of what your business is.

When you develop a great logo, you can benefit from this simple tool in many ways:

1. Your logo will become a surrogate for your business, and will become well known so that when people see your logo, they see you.

2. Your logo will get you noticed.

3. Your logo will help you pre-educate prospective clients on what you do.

4. Your logo will help to create strong name recognition.

To create a personal logo, you need to be simple. It can be as easy as your name or business name in a cool font, or it can be as sophisticated as some of the high-powered corporation logos. But if you are trying to get your money's worth from your logo, then you should try to find a personal logo that will have all three of the essentials for a good logo: a name, a slogan, and an icon. The name is simply your business name. It is on all the printed and virtual items that you use, and you use it in all sorts of ways that you may not even realize.

Choosing the Right Name

So, why is it that so many businesses out there seem to mess it up? They either try to impersonate the larger corporate businesses or

CHAPTER 4: PERSONALIZE IT ALL: LOGOS, BROCHURES, AND WEB SITES

they do not think that their company's name is important. But, your company name is the most important part of your business. It has the potential to instantly identify what you do, who you are, and what your business stands for. So take your time on your business name, or reevaluate it if you think you may have spent too little time on it.

When you are naming your business, make sure you do not have anything similar to another business competitor. You want to be completely different from your competition, so take a look at the names of your major competitors. You will probably find that about 90 percent of your competitors, both large and small, have similar names. Do not follow this example! Create your own name that is both unique and still states who you are and what you do. There are some exceptions to this, as some businesses have a strict culture on their names, so they do all look similar. For example, law firms all hold the names of their partners or the main attorney in the firm. It is the culture of law firms to name their practices in this way, so it is hard to avoid this.

You can always opt to name your business after yourself. In about 90 percent of cases, this is the right way to go with your business name. You want people to do business with you, not with a large corporation, and your clients will want to know that they are doing business with a person and not a huge business. When you use your name as your company's name, you create a great familiarity with your clients and with your target market. You also use your reputation to help build up your business, and people who know you will automatically know what type of business you have.

Now, do not fret over creating a corporate-sounding name so your business will look more important. Most business owners actually fall into this mindset. Companies do this to capitalize on the credibility of larger corporations, but in today's business market, there is not a lot of good credibility in a large corporation-like name. Most consumers assume that a big corporation will only have them dealing with an automated machine that cannot help if they have a problem.

If you use your personal name for your company, you do not have to use this name for your personal brand, and vice versa. Take Henry Ford for example; when he started out, his brand was Henry Ford. But this brand has now turned into Ford, and the name is so familiar that people instantly know what Ford is and what they stand for. The late Walt Disney is also a great example of this name branding that has shortened over time. While the brand has changed since its inception, the principles, the passion, and the vision are all still the same for both of these companies.

So, when you are ready to create a business name, start with yourself. Add in some other elements if you like, that will help to identify your skills, education, business, and so on. Here are some examples of names that are perfect for their chosen business (these names are all fictional):

1. Bob Smith LLC
2. John Doe Design Studio
3. Italian Catering by Tony Lasorda
4. E. J. Martin Chiropractic
5. Sue Edwards Realtors

All of these business names incorporate a person's name into the business name, and most communicate exactly what they do.

CHAPTER 4: PERSONALIZE IT ALL: LOGOS, BROCHURES, AND WEB SITES

There are a few guidelines that you should try to stick to when you are creating your business name, as they will help you create the right name for you:

1. Try to describe what your business does in one or two words, such as "Design Studio," "Italian Catering," or "Realtors."

2. For conservative companies, such as financial services, you should try to use your name and "LLC" or "Company" to keep your business professional.

3. If you choose to use only your name, create a slogan that tells what you do and who you are. Place this slogan after your name on marketing material, business cards, Web sites, and so on.

4. If you have a longer formal name, but you use a familiar version, then use the familiar version in your business name. For example, if your name is Robert J. Smith II, but everyone calls you Bob Smith, then use that name in your business, such as "Bob Smith LLC."

5. Try to stay away from two overused adages: "… & Company" and "… & Associates." These have been used for so long that they no longer carry the true meaning that they once did.

Finding the Right Slogan

Your business slogan is included in your personal logo. Most people can easily identify several different slogans that they hear on a regular basis and are familiar with. For example, "Like a

Rock" was used by Chevrolet for many years, and is still associated with their company, even when they use a different slogan.

A company will create a slogan for three distinct reasons: to inform consumers about their products or services, to convey an emotion to the consumers that they want them to associate with their product, or to motivate consumers to take action. But you are not creating a huge corporation; you are simply creating a slogan for your business. These corporations have millions to put into marketing their business and products, so they hire people to create these slogans for them. New business owners, small business owners, and most business owners in general do not have this kind of money to use for a slogan. These large corporations can also use very obscure slogans that only convey an emotion, because they have the marketing dollars to buy ads, send out mail, and build locations all over to let consumers know what they do. Smaller businesses cannot afford this luxury. So, when you are creating a slogan for your business, you need to do one of two things: tell people what you do and who you do it for, or tell people what you do and the benefits of doing business with you.

Here are a couple of examples of telling people what you do and who you do it for:

1. Web Consulting for Business Professionals

2. Massage Therapy for Expectant Mothers

Here are a couple of examples of telling people what you do and the benefits of doing business with you:

1. Retirement Planning for Your Future

2. Designing Fashions to Help You Look Like a Star

Make sure to keep your slogan simple. You do not need an extremely long one to convey your business to consumers, and they will not have the time to stop and read a paragraph. The average consumer only takes about one to two seconds to read a slogan, so it has to be short and simple. Try not to go over eight words at the most, and keep it as simple as you can. Your potential clients should be able to look at your slogan and instantly know what you do and if you are right for them or not; you must grab their attention quickly. Here are a few other tips to use when you are creating your business's slogan:

1. Test out your slogan on people and gauge the responses. If you do not like what you hear back, keep changing it around until you do.

2. It is not a good idea to put your slogan in quotes, bold, or italic print. Most people do this because they assume it adds an air of drama to their slogan, but it does not.

3. Make sure that your grammar and spelling are perfect. Any mistakes, no matter how small, can make your business look less than professional.

4. Avoid using "solutions" in your slogan. This is a word that is overused in the business world, and you should steer clear of it at all costs.

5. Make sure that your slogan is specific and says what you do with precision.

Creating the Perfect Icon

The graphic element that will go into your logo is your icon. Not all logos have them, but if you can find the right one, then you will immediately increase your visibility and the effectiveness of your logo. For example, if you own a body shop that prefers to work on older, classic cars, you can create (or have created) a simple drawing of your favorite classic car to go into your logo. When potential customers see your logo, they will automatically know that you love classic cars from a specific era, without ever reading your slogan. This also gives both potential clients and current clients a personal connection with you and your business.

An icon can be anything at all. From a monogram of your business initials to a graphic design to a photo, anything at all that conveys your business interests, your profession, or your passion can be used as an icon for your logo. But there are a few icons that you should avoid like the plague if you can help it. Cliché icons that everyone in your profession uses are to be avoided at all costs. These include some of the following: a house for real estate agents, a quill or pencil for writers, a computer for any type of computer or Web business, or a chef's hat for a catering or food service. These are all icons that have been overused by these professions and now only result in making your business logo look like an amateur created it.

Here are some other tips to help you choose the right icon for your logo:

1. If you use a photo, make sure that you test it out in a small size and in black and white to see if it will reproduce well. If not, move on to your next choice. Most photos do not reproduce well, so you may consider this as a last resort.

2. Keep your icon in your target market. For example, if you are a stamp collector, you should not put a stamp on your logo if you are marketing to a children's market.

3. If you are not artistically inclined, find a professional artist to help you. There are plenty of sites on the Web where you can hire freelancers to create a single image or icon for you. Do-it-yourself icons do not have the best appeal unless you are a graphic designer or artist.

4. Whatever you do, do not use a family crest as an icon. First, the graphics will not reproduce well and second, the detail will not look good on an extremely small icon.

Putting Your Logo Together Correctly

Now that you have looked over all the elements that go into creating a good logo, it is time to put it all together. Make sure you have picked out all the elements that you want, you have tested them with family and friends to see how they work, and you are completely ready to move forward.

It is now time to put them all together in your business logo.

When you are putting the pieces together, you want your logo to appear to be one graphic that blends together well. You do not want three different elements that are choppy, do not overlap well, or look like they were just pasted together.

The normal place to start is with your company name. The name should dominate the logo, and your slogan should run under your name. When you are ready to start, there are several different areas that you need to consider when you are placing and designing the name typeset:

1. **Color** — You should only choose two to three colors for your logo and no more. Start with the most common neutral colors that a lot of businesses choose: white, black,

or gray. Then, move on to one of the other five main colors that are great in a logo: blue, green, orange, red, or yellow. If you like, you can use a variation of one of the five main colors, such as purple, gold, or aqua. These colors all print well and will give an emotion to your logo. Do not use too many colors or odd variations, as these do not always print well, and do not always look the same on different printers. Here are some of the emotions and the reasons that you should stick with the five main colors or only a couple of variations of them: The eye focuses red colors behind the retina and makes the reds seem to move toward the viewer. The eye focuses blue colors in front of the retina and makes the blues seem to be farther away from the viewer. Reds stand for excitement and energy, while blues stand for peace and relaxation. You should always consider what emotions you want to convey in your logo and then match up the colors that fit that the emotion. In *The 22 Immutable Laws of Branding* by Al and Laura Ries, the authors break down what the main logo colors convey to consumers:

1. Red = Attention

2. Yellow = Caution

3. Green = Nature

4. Blue = Leadership

5. Purple = Royalty

6. Black = Luxury

7. White = Purity

2. **Typeface** — There are two different kinds of typeface that you need to choose from when creating your logo: serif, which are the old-fashioned typesets that you see in newspapers, and sans serif, which are the newer, sleeker typesets that do not have all the fancy additions. When you are choosing your typeface, make sure you consider how readable these are at smaller sizes. Also, consider that some computers and printers may not have the correct typeset that you choose (if you choose a newer font), so your logo may not come out right if printed somewhere else. It is always good to stick with tried and true fonts that almost every computer and printer is familiar with: Times, Arial, Optima, Garamond, or Goudy. If you are going for a more traditional feel for your logo, then you may consider the serif typefaces as they promote an old-fashioned feel and are normally used for conservative businesses. But if you are going for a more modern feel for your logo, then go with the sans serif typefaces, since they are used by more modern businesses. Overall, choose a typeset that you like. You can even choose one for your name and one for your slogan as long as you make sure that both are readable at small sizes. And, never use all capitals in a name or logo unless your name is initials. This comes across as shouting at the consumer.

3. **Size** — Now, you need to determine how big or small your logo should be. Get the three items together for your logo and choose your colors and fonts, then you may head to a professional to help you determine the right size for your logo. A professional graphic design software can help put together all your components and size them so that are readable and clear. This is why you want to make sure to keep your logo simple; anything that is too complex in

your logo will turn into a blob when it is small, and size does matter when it comes to a logo. You should make sure your logo and slogan will look good on a business card and still be readable, but it should also look good on stationery or brochures at a 2 ½ by 1 ½ inch size.

Put My Logo Where?

Now that you have your logo, you have sized it up, colored it in, and it looks as perfect as it can get, it is time to incorporate it into your business and onto everything. Make sure when you are placing your logo on business materials that you use the same colors, typeset, and font sizes in other printed materials so that everything matches and looks professional. Here are some places you need to consider placing your logo:

- Brochures
- Postcards
- Direct mail
- Letterhead
- Labels
- Envelopes
- Invoices
- Web site
- Print or TV advertising
- Outdoor advertising

- T-shirts or caps

- PowerPoint presentations

- On your door or windows at your offices

- Any organization or event that you sponsor

Now that you have your logo perfected, you can move on to the brochure — an item that no business can be without!

Brochure Time

Now that you have your logo, you can begin work on other areas of your business tools that will be passed out to clients and potential clients to bring them into your fold. The first major tool that you will use is a business brochure.

Most people hear the word "brochure" and automatically think about a trifold, three panel, glossy item that sits all over your doctor's offices. Or, they see those amateur brochures that people create and print out on their printer at home, filled with sales information, and can put you to sleep.

But when you have a great brochure, you can give it out instead of your business cards and provide people with more information right away. When you take the time to create a great brochure that will stand out from the others, such as with an unusual shape, a professional quality, and a full-color layout, then your brochure becomes a great prospecting tool and no longer just a sales tool.

A prospecting tool? That is right. A great personal brochure for your business can become more than a simple sales tool that everyone sees. If you make the investment to create a great brochure, you then can use it as a prospecting tool to pass out to prospective clients. This type of brochure is used for building rapport and not completely for selling. This is a way to get your personal story and position across to the readers.

A good personal brochure will have two distinctive jobs: to get your prospective clients to know you and to get your prospective clients to trust you. To get clients to know you means to have them understand a bit about you as well as your business. This does not mean this is a brag page, highlighting your education or training; that is for a sales brochure. A personal brochure is to help your prospective clients feel a deeper connection to you, so you break through the natural resistance to a salesperson by not selling to them. When you create the copy for your personal brochure, you should place items such as anecdotes from your childhood, achievements (not sales orientated), life lessons, and so on. Nothing that ties in with sales goes in these brochures.

Now that you understand the first job of a personal brochure, the second job is to get your prospective clients to trust you. This is not as much about the contents of the brochure as it is about the overall look and feel of it. Remember a time when a salesperson handed you a cheaply made brochure that looked like they created it themselves in their spare time. Chances are that you did not purchase anything from them, and you probably headed out the door. Now think about when someone handed you a professionally made, beautiful brochure that was done on expensive paper. It probably did not matter if you wanted to buy what they were selling or not; if you did not buy from them, you entertained the idea and listened to all they had to say, did you not? Quality over quantity is the rule when it comes to personal brochures.

CHAPTER 4: PERSONALIZE IT ALL: LOGOS, BROCHURES, AND WEB SITES

So what is your current brochure like, if you already have one? Does it fall into that first category, with the cheap paper and the total sales lines? Or does it fall into that second category, with the beautifully laid-out photos and the professional feel? Does is embarrass you to hand out your brochures or are you happy to give them anytime, anywhere?

If you are not sure how to create a great brochure, have no fear. There are a few steps that you need to be sure to follow when you are creating your personal brochure in order to create a winner every time instead of the loser that people trash right away. If you are not a writer, graphic designer, or other creative professional, then creating a great personal brochure is probably giving you a sick feeling in the pit of your stomach. But I am going to share six steps with you that will help you get past that sick feeling and regain the feeling that you can do this. If you stick with these steps, you will find that you can create a great personal brochure that will become one of the strongest personal branding tools in your arsenal.

The First Step

The first step to creating a winning personal brochure is to choose a single attribute to promote. You cannot be everything to everyone, so do not try. Your objective in creating a good personal brochure is to convey your brand in a way that strikes an emotional chord but is clear to the reader at the same time. This is why you want to choose one thing to focus on, since you cannot make your meaning clear if you are jumping to a different topic in each paragraph. When you are choosing your topic, find the most compelling way that you provide a great value to your clients and make it your focus. Keep in mind that your brochure is not about selling; it is all about breaking down the resistance to sales by informing the potential client about you and your business.

The Second Step

The second step to creating a winning personal brochure is to take the time to map out your story. Since you are the product that you are selling to the potential client, you should be the focus of the brochure. The soul of your brochure is a minibiography that will tell your story and allow the reader to see a bit further into you and why you do what you do.

Think of the way pushy salespeople make you feel when you enter a store or a car lot; you know that they are already trying to push you to purchase something. This makes you want to run the other way. Remember this feeling when you are creating your personal brochure. Instead of pushing your reader to buy something, you want to make them comfortable, like you are old friends, catching up on old times. You want to come across as another human being, not a salesperson, which is done by talking about your accomplishments and not what you are selling. By helping your readers to see that you are not selling them anything, but simply letting them know who you are, you are building the trust that you will need in order to gain their business and their referrals.

Your story should consist of 80 to 90 percent of the brochure. Since this is a "soft sell," where you are more important than what you are selling, do not place any sales information at all in this brochure. Keep in mind that your readers are not dumb, and they will quickly figure out what type of business you have. So, if you place any type of sales information in your brochure, it will have no credibility and will take away from what you are trying to accomplish. But if you hand your potential client a brochure that is only about you and what you stand for, it will be a complete surprise and be completely unexpected.

When you are thinking of things to put in your brochure, here are some great items to use: where and how you grew up, good family stories that involve you or your parents' raising of you, your education (be careful with this one though, and do not put too much into your brochure about it), any major life experiences that help to make you the person you are today, what your first jobs were and what you learned from them, and any mentors that you have or life lessons that you have learned.

You may be doubting that this will work. After all, a brochure is a sales tool, right? Well, think about when the Olympics are on television. In between the events, there are all sorts of advertisements about the athletes themselves, stories about them overcoming some problem to get where they are. No matter if you like that person or hate them, you watch their story because it is about overcoming an obstacle. Everyone can identify with that, as all people have to overcome something in their lifetime. As long as you keep in mind that people like to hear personal stories about triumph over tragedy, then your brochure will be a hit.

The Third Step

When you are ready to write out the copy for your personal brochure, take the time to find a professional writer to do it if you are not a writer. It is worth the money, and it will give your brochure a polished feel and let readers know that you are a professional.

Here are some guidelines to stick to when you are creating your personal brochure copy:

1. Do not use a first-person voice. Always use third person, even when you are writing about yourself. When a reader reads something that is written in the third person, they consider the source to be reliable since they will be writing objectively.

2. You can use a first-person voice when you are talking about personal experiences, but you should place this information in quotations if the rest of your brochure is written in the third person. If you use the first person too much in your brochure, you will come across as bragging to the reader, which is not good.

3. Keep the copy positive throughout. You do not want to dwell on bad stories or anything negative in your brochure.

4. Use paragraphs for your copy, not bullets. Bullets seem like you are selling something, while paragraphs create a story.

5. Be honest and candid with the reader. Consumers seem to carry with them a personal lie detector and will be able to instantly see though anything that you put into the brochure that is not true or is exaggerated.

6. Avoid clichés like they are going out of style (for example). You should avoid clichés whenever you can so you do not sound corny.

7. Subheadings should be used to help break up the text. These short headlines that are placed between the major areas of your brochure copy will help to make your brochure easier to read. Make your subheadings powerful so they will be interesting to the reader.

8. Create a strong, grabbing headline that will provide more emotional value to your brochure.

9. Keep your brochure short. Usually between 250 to 500 words will do the trick, and will leave your reader wanting to know more about you, not tired of hearing about you.

The Fourth Step

Your fourth step will be to either create or have a graphic designer create a "knock 'em dead" cover for you. It will not matter how eloquent your written copy is if your cover stinks. Without a great cover, people will not even want to pick it up, much less open it to see what it says.

Get with a good graphic designer to help you create a cover that will scream "Read Me!" to people when they see it. You should choose an image that will help to stop your readers and compel them to open the brochure to see what you have to say. You also need that great headline to complement the cover so that your readers are intrigued to open it up.

When you are creating your cover, do not place any images on it that relate to your business or what you sell. If you do, they will smell that you are trying to sell them something and they will put it down right away. Instead of promoting your business or services, your cover should create an air of mystery — something that will strike curiosity into your reader. But do not put your company name or logo on the cover. It should always go on the back.

Along the same lines with the cover, you need to have a graphic designer help you to create a clean but attractive to a reader. Keep plenty of "white space" in your brochure, where there is nothing at all — no text, no graphics. You do not have to fill every inch of space in your brochure to get your point across, and the right spacing and clean look will be more appealing to your readers.

For any photos that you want to place in your brochure, always have a professional do them. This means you do not use the school photos you took as a kid, you do not get your best friend to take them (unless they are a professional photographer), and you do not use any type of amateur photos at all. Remember that "a picture is worth a thousand words," so the quality of your photos will add credibility to your brochure and to yourself.

There is one thing to always remember — no head shots. These are great for yearbooks and company information, but not for your personal brochure.

The Fifth Step

The fifth step is to choose your brochure size. But first you need to throw out all of the normal sizes that you have ever seen.

The size of your brochure should be completely unique. Do not go with the regular 8 ½ by 11 format that will fit into a normal legal envelope. These are way too easy to throw away, so you should always go with the abnormal sizes, such as a larger square brochure. Anything that stands out from the rest of the pack will be noticed immediately and will always get picked up and read. A square brochure is actually the best, because most people will think of it as an invitation and will be more likely to read it.

You should also consider which type of fold you want for your brochure. A good graphic designer can help you with this, since there are several to choose from, or you can create a custom fold.

The Sixth Step

Your sixth step is to spend the money for high-quality printing. You want a brochure that is of high quality, on a good, glossy paper that will communicate that you are a professional and you go out of your way for your clients. Make sure your printer does your brochure in full color, so no photos are lost or changed by less than normal colors.

Find an experienced printer that can do the typesetting for you, and you should not always go with the lowest cost on this. If you are looking to save a few pennies, then you need to cut costs another way, not here. After all, you are looking for a printer that can create a great work for you to be proud of, not something that you spent so much time and money on, and are embarrassed to show.

Always opt for the heavy, higher-quality paper, usually at least 100-pound glossy cover stock. When it comes to how many to print, start with around 2,500. And, you should not do what some other business owners do: horde your brochures away so you never pass them out. Some people think that they spent all this money on them, and they are beautiful, too beautiful to give out, so they sit and collect dust and never get to accomplish what they were designed for.

Great Uses for Your New Brochures

Now that you have designed and printed a wonderful brochure that showcases you and what you stand for, and you have finally stopped staring at it, it is time to put it to work for you. Keep in mind that personal brochures are in no way direct mailers. These are too expensive and they should go to people you have already met in your networking time.

When you are ready to send or give them out, here are some places that you should consider passing them out:

1. Always pass out a copy of your personal brochure to anyone who is remotely associated with you or your business. This includes: business associates, colleagues, any media contacts you have, friends, and other business contacts.

2. Mail out two copies to your current clients — the first one is for them, and the second one they will pass on to someone else.

3. Mail out a copy to any prospect in your database that you have met during your networking, but make sure to include a cover letter.

4. Give out ten to twelve copies to any professionals that are good referral sources for you. Encourage them to pass them out, and offer an incentive for them if they do.

5. Use your personal brochures instead of business cards when you are at a networking event.

6. Hand your brochure out at speaking events.

7. Hand your brochure out at seminars in your information package.

8. Include your brochure in any press kits you send out.

9. Carry them with you to trade shows and pass them out to contacts you meet.

10. Pass out your brochures at trade shows to every visitor that comes to your booth.

With your logo and brochure ready to go, you need to work on developing a Web presence for your business. Web design is our next step, and a vital one in today's online market.

Web Design Time

Now that we have gone through the logos and the brochures that you can use to spark your business, it is time to consider your Web site. In today's crazy online business world, you have to have a Web site. This is the tool that almost every contact will expect you to have next to a business card. You have probably already had someone ask you what your business's Web address is if you have been in business very long. The Web is a great way to reach people, since they can browse your site and learn about you and your company before they decide to invest their time or money with you.

So you are in one of two places right now: Either you do not have a Web site, or you have one and you need to improve it. Either way, you can start to worry about the cost of designing and maintaining a Web site, but do not worry. There are numerous ways that you can create and maintain a great business Web site that will not cost much, which include software that will design nearly the entire site for you.

Before you surf online to find one of these companies, you should know why you need a site, what your target market can benefit from your business site, and how you can use your site to spread your new brand. It does not matter if you are simply changing your current site or if you are creating one from scratch. You need a personal Web site as well as a business one.

Reasons to Be Online

There are three main reasons that your business, and you, should have a major online presence:

1. A Web site will build up your credibility. Your Web site is a public relations tool, not a sales tool, and it will help establish you as a real person and your business as a real company. No matter how many people work for you, you can always polish up a Web site so it will give great credibility to you and your business and increase your trustworthiness in the eyes of your clients. Also, most people assume that if you have a Web site, you have a legitimate company. So it gives people a way to check and be sure that you are not just a scam artist.

2. A Web site will capture leads for you. If you create a site that has great copy and content that will prompt people to look further into your business, then you have a great tool that will automatically capture leads for you.

3. A Web site will help to maintain your relationships. Your Web site is a great platform for you to stay in touch with contacts and clients. You can send them email, post information on your Web site about special events, and you can bring them on the site for special promotions and more. Entrepreneurs are taking advantage of a business Web site, so do not be left out.

Benefits of a Web Site

While it involves some work to set one up, having a Web site is worth the trouble, and you can easily launch a beautiful site that will portray exactly who you are and what you do. A Web site can transform your home-based office into a large company, since people surfing the Web will not know you are sitting at home in your pajamas working, and not at a large office building assigning projects.

A good Web site will give you ultimate control over the first impression of yourself and your business. It is a powerful tool, and it can do a lot for you. Here are some of the great benefits that a Web site can do for you:

1. Give new contacts a way to check you out and learn all about you without feeling pressured to buy from you.

2. Help to extend your brand to people all over the United States and the world.

3. It gives your clients immediate access to information about you, your business, and more.

4. It gives you a great platform to launch email campaigns to let everyone know about your business promotions, news, or other items.

5. It can help you build your database through visitor information.

6. It can distribute literature for you, without costing you a penny in printing.

7. It can be an immediate storefront, so anyone with a credit card can purchase your services.

8. It can increase your visibility and credibility by giving you an online presence.

Now that you have mastered these areas — logo, brochures, and Web design — you can begin to focus your efforts on other areas that you can extend your brand to.

Chapter 5: Extending Your Brand

For a business to become successful, you need to be able to develop ways to extend your brand into as many other areas as possible. Advertisements in a newspaper or magazine, letters to groups that fall into your target market, referrals from your top customers, and monthly email newsletters are great ways of putting your brand into other areas. These different areas are called "branding channels" and they are the routes by which your business information gets from you to your target VIP clients. To be able to use these branding channels to your advantage, you need to understand what they are and how they work.

What Are Branding Channels?

Just as navigation channels carry ships to their destinations, branding channels carry your business information — such as your values, specialization, position, and abilities — to your target market and beyond. Once you have created a personal brand, as well as the specialty and positioning that go along with it, your brand will reach your potential clients through your branding channels.

But, these are also specialized marketing channels that are used to create new business opportunities, bring in new clients, and more. These channels also communicate the essence of your personal brand, everything you do, how you do it, the value you bring to your clients, your philosophies, and everything about your business and brand. Plus, these channels communicate all of this to some of the most influential people in marketing.

Eight Major Branding Channels

There is no limit to the ways that you can bring your brand and your message to your target market. Just to be clear though, we have broken down the most cost effective and useful branding channels into eight major channels that make up 95 percent of the branding work that you will ever have to do. As you get further into developing your personal brand and gain experience in promoting it, then you will naturally start to move toward the channels that will fit your business and your personal style. But it is important to have a quick list of them all, just in case.

Here are the eight major channels, and some smaller categories that go into each, that you should always consider:

1. Referrals From Clients

    a. Referral requests from your best clients

    b. Personal brochures

    c. Premium offers for referrals

2. Referrals From Other Business Professionals

    a. Referral requests from your best business contacts

b. Rewards or incentives

c. Endorsements by letter or email

3. Direct Mail Marketing

    a. Sales letters

    b. Catalogs

    c. Personal postcards

    d. Mailing calendars

4. Networking

    a. Business cards

    b. Personal brochures

5. Seminars

    a. Personal brochures

    b. Seminar manuals

    c. PowerPoint presentations

6. Public Relations

    a. Media kits

    b. Press releases

    c. Editor relationship programs

    d. Sponsorships

7. Warm Calls

    a. Phone scripts

    b. Product and services information kits

8. Web Site Marketing

    a. E-newsletters

    b. Product and services special offers

Secondary Branding Channels

There are some other branding channels that you might want to consider, but they only work for about 5 percent of the companies that actually use them. This is because they will require large budgets and longer exposure to help create brand awareness in a target market. So, more than likely, your money will be better spent in the eight major branding channels. But here is the list of the secondary ones, just in case:

1. Print Advertising

    a. Display advertisements

    b. Classified advertisements

    c. Yellow Pages advertisements

2. Outdoor Advertising

    a. Billboards

    b. Bus benches

c. Airport signs

3. Radio Advertising

   a. Host-paid radio show

   b. Commercials

   c. Infomercials

4. Television Advertising

   a. Host-paid TV show

   b. Pay-for-guest TV show

   c. Commercials

   d. Infomercials

5. Trade Shows and Special Events

   a. Booth

   b. Premiums

   c. Products and services literature

   d. Banners

Creating Ways to Reach Your Target Market

When you are building your personal brand, consistency and repetition will have to take over. Repeating your branding messages over and over — continually using only the same methods — can backfire on you and become ineffective, and annoy the people that you are trying to reach. This is why those who are experienced brand builders utilize multiple channels, and coordinate them to work together to help drive the brand and message home. It is similar to attacking the same target over and over; you have to make sure that you do it from different directions so your chance of success goes up.

You must obey the Rule of Five when you are trying to maximize the effectiveness of your marketing. The Rule of Five is this: You must employ at least five channels to reach your target market. If you deploy them so they all complement each other, then you will have a better chance that they will coincide and work well together to completely get your marketing message across to your target market.

But does this really work? Well, think about how you make a decision to purchase something, like a new car for example. Do you make your decision based on one single ad you saw? Usually not. You will see an ad, see a different ad a few days later, see that your best friend bought that car, and then see a news story on the Internet. All of these different channels are used to get your attention on several different levels and get you constantly thinking about that particular brand of car. They all work well together to convince you to purchase that car.

Keep Your Marketing "Synergized"

The inexperienced marketers will think of only one tool to use to get their business brand out on the market. One tool, one goal, and they never reach that goal. Experienced marketers will place an ad in the paper to generate calls or emails, send out a press release about every month or so to generate their company's name in print, and send out direct emails to their clients about special referral bonuses they offer, along with other special promotions and marketing tactics. But to actually get your money's worth, you have to think like a professional personal brander. You have to get your channels feeding into each other and working together. You have to create synergy with your marketing campaigns and keep them "synergized."

This means the whole of your marketing campaign is more important than the sum of its parts. When you are designing a branding campaign and using several channels in a "synergized" way, you will get two unique results that will help your business get the message across. The two results that you will get are: each different channel will drive home your message by itself, and each different channel will increase the effectiveness of the others.

Take this example: Say you are holding a public seminar to promote your graphic design business, which is your first channel. At this seminar, you give out copies of your personal brochure (which is your second channel), and explain the contents to visitors. This brochure will lead those people to your Web site for more information about you and your business, which is channel three. After this seminar, you will send out reminder emails to the people who registered when they attended, and direct mail to those who did not attend, but registered, which is channel four. You also recorded the seminar and you send audiotapes to your local radio stations, television stations, and newspapers with some brochures and invitations to attend your next seminar to do a story about you, which is channel five. Now you have reached the five channels you wanted to achieve, and they all go hand-in-hand with each other. This is how you work your channels together to hit your target market with several different chances to respond to you and your business.

As you continue to learn about the different channels and put together your specific marketing campaign, always think about how you can integrate your channels together and use them to make other channels better.

There Are No Bad Branding Channels

Branding channels are like race cars. They are only as good as the person driving them on the track. Every branding channel will work, just like a race car, but the question is, is the channel right for your business to use?

Look at this example of a bad branding channel use and a good branding channel use:

John Smith is a retirement advisor who is trying to target widows who are nearing their retirement age of 65. He started off using seminars to target this group, and found that he got a bad response from them. This was a bad branding channel for him.

So, he did some research. He found that most widows who are over the age of 60 would much rather find a retirement advisor whom they trusted and felt comfortable with, not someone they had never met who was feeding them a lot of information they did not understand.

He changed his branding channel to sponsoring a weekly card tournament at the senior citizens' center in town. He even helped to run the tournament and provided napkins, score cards, and other items with his name, business information, and phone number on them.

Once he changed his branding channel, he found that his business began to soar since his target market trusted him and knew him.

They also began sending him several referrals each, which helped his business to continue to grow.

This is only an example of how a good branding channel can flop with certain businesses. You will need to be creative if your first choices of branding channels do not work. Keep in mind that there are no bad branding channels; they are only as good as the person driving them.

The Main Categories of Branding Channels

Within branding channels, there are two main categories: inclusive and exclusive.

- Inclusive channels are those where you will not have much control over who sees the message. You will probably attract a larger response, but will gain lower-quality clients who may not fit into your VIP filters. This will work for building seminar attendance and mailing lists, but you will have work on the back end to weed out those clients who are not part of your VIP list.

- Exclusive channels are those where you have a lot of control over who sees the message. You will get a smaller response, but you will reach your target VIP clients almost 99 percent of the time. This is great to whittle down those massive client lists into smaller, VIP lists.

Inclusive Channels

There are several different forms of inclusive channels that you can use to pull in clients to your business. Keep in mind that these will be seen by more people, but may not bring in all the VIP clients you are seeking. This section will go through some of the inclusive channels and their good points and bad points:

Seminars — Since seminars take a lot of time and planning, and you need to be able to get up in front of a group and talk, they may not be for you. Some businesses are not seminar ready, which means they are not right for seminar-style presentations. But, about 80 percent of businesses are in a type of business where these would help them. This means the chances are good that when you are ready to try your business hand at a seminar, they will probably help you bring in a lot of clients.

In seminars, you automatically have a captive audience and market. Even without charging an admission, you can give your audience a great sales pitch that is disguised as an education in what your business is. The whole idea behind a seminar is to deliver your brand message in person to a big group, and then try to get as many of that group to meet with you individually at a later time. Seminars are also a great way to distribute materials and information to your target market.

There are actually a couple of different types of seminars that your business can hold:

1. **Private seminars** — These help you to promote a company, the Chamber of Commerce, or another group, and these help you to get a smaller group that you can prescreen to fit into your VIP client list. These seminars will be more demanding, and will require a lot more detailed work on your part, but will allow you better business contacts and allow you to market to the people attending the seminar.

2. **Public seminars** — These are seminars that you advertise in the community and that anyone can come to. These are usually for building a networking basis and bring in a lot of people, even though they may be less desirable than your VIP clients.

Seminars are good for: making a lot of face-to-face contacts that you can market your personal brand to, getting a chance to sell large groups of prospects on your specific skills and services, distributing literature, gaining contact information, and making appointments with potential customers that will usually lead to sales.

Seminars are bad for: saving money on advertising (the advertising and hall space for a seminar are usually high), filtering your VIP clients out from the crowd, and saving time on marketing and advertising, as they can be quite long.

Seminars can work with other branding channels by allowing you to: hand out information to all those that attend (including things like your personal brochure and articles about you), tell people about other events that you are hosting, get addresses or email addresses for direct mail marketing, use the seminar for a press release opportunity to get your name in the media, and to make some initial contacts that will turn your cold calls into warm ones.

To use a seminar effectively, you should know what kind of target market you want, practice your public speaking, provide good quality information and handouts, keep your seminar in the one-hour range, promote upcoming seminars or events, and make sure everyone leaves with some of your printed materials.

Public Relations (PR) — PR work involves using the media to produce coverage of your business and yourself, as well as outside activities, like charity work and other sponsorships. There is a lot more to media than you probably think, such as television, local newspapers, radio, magazines, cable television stations, local network affiliates, online media, and even trade publications that cover only your area of business.

PR work also involves sponsorship of special causes, such as Little League and charity events. These are a great way to attach goodwill to your name while getting your name in front of a large group of people in your community and abroad.

Normally, PR work means using the press for press releases and follow-up to generate coverage for your business. The goal is to get news briefs, calendar listings, or even features done on your business either in a printed media or on a broadcast all about you and your business. Good PR work also means you need to cultivate good relationships with journalists based on a mutual benefit. You should get to know the print and broadcast editors and reporters in your area and the editors at trade magazines that cover your field.

PR is good for: being one of the most powerful branding tools around, its cheap cost (usually it is free), its credibility, the wide coverage that it has, increasing public visibility and awareness of your business and who you are, the pre-notion that if a business is featured in an unbiased news medium you have to be good, and it is great to help create awareness of special events like seminars, charity sports, and so on.

PR is bad for: producing strong, consistent, regular exposure. Also, you will not have any control over the editors and you cannot guarantee that the coverage you will get will go from week to week, or month to month.

PR can work with other branding channels by: creating a higher awareness of your business and you which makes networking and referrals easier, driving target market clients to your seminars or special events, helping to promote specific projects for your business, and turning you into a local celebrity which helps with your advertising,

To use PR effectively, you should: form good relationships with editors and journalists, send a Rolodex card with a great cover letter to the editors to introduce yourself to them as an "expert source" in your field, write a column for a local newspaper or publication, learn and follow the standard press-release formats, send press releases when you have news, even if it is just a new hire.

The Web — The Internet is a great, easy-to-use branding channel that allows you to have a simple site with useful information and features to help give you a 24-hour information source for your clients. This branding center helps your clients and potential clients access your business any time they want. It is powerful and can be used to a great advantage — you can control your users' information, experience, and their ability to extract information from your site, and you can drive in your personal branding message with graphics, great ad copy, and more. If your Web site is done right, it will be an extremely powerful tool for building your brand name with potential clients, media contacts, and other influential people in the world.

The Web is good for: serving as an all-hours storefront and information center for anyone who wants to know more about you and your business, offering special pricing for online visitors to drive in more sales, giving prospective clients a no-hassle way to check out your business and what you have to offer, and offer free information related to your business and field.

The Web is bad for: filtering out VIP clients. You will get tons of hits from people all over the world, but you will not be able to filter them with the special VIP filters that you put into place earlier. It is also not useful for those clients who have slow connections, do not use the Web often, or clients who are technophobic.

The Web can work with other branding channels by: allowing people to download versions of your brochures, promoting special events (like seminars), giving editors and other media personnel a quick, easy way to learn about you and your business for a story, getting visitors to your site to sign up for a free newsletter to help increase your direct mail list, giving people who are referred to you a free place to check out your business and you before they meet you in person, and allowing you to do more online polls for those who attend your seminars to find out how you can change your seminars for the better.

The Web can be used more effectively by: hiring a professional Web designer or technical programmer to do your business's Web site, promoting your Web site in all of your marketing, referring new contacts to your Web site, creating fresh content and articles so users will have a reason to come back constantly, keeping a privacy policy posted so that users will feel more confident in your business and in giving you their information, and making your site less about the bells and whistles and more about you and your business.

Advertising — There are plenty of different things that fall under advertising: billboards, Yellow Pages ads, radio station commercials, and Web banners. Most people will oversaturate their local market with advertising and not realize they can be focusing their efforts elsewhere. We take a different approach to advertising and tell you not to use local advertising until you have gotten most of the benefits out of the other areas of branding channels. That is right — do not use your local advertising until you have maxed out your other branding channels. Why, you ask? Advertising is expensive, and will require months of exposure before a client comes into your office. So, your money is better spent elsewhere right now.

Whenever your personal brand is firmly established though, a great advertising campaign is a great way to spread the awareness of your business locally, and help to firm your hold on the target market you are trying to reach. There is a large intimidation factor that goes along with advertising, and it can make your competitors think twice before they try to take you on in a market that you have a firm grasp on.

What advertising is good for: reaching huge groups of people without much effort on your part. You simply place an ad and wait. The ad will be seen by up to 100,000 people within a few days or less, and you will start to see the benefits. It is a great way to let people know your name, your business, and what you do.

What advertising is not good for: reaching that special VIP target market and controlling the leads that come in. Once you put an ad out to the public, it is fair game and both the VIP clients and the other type will come rolling through your door. The only way to avoid this is to put the ad in a targeted trade publication, which can cost you more money than a normal publication. Even then, you will still get some people who do not fit into your VIP list. It is also easy to create ads that will "pull" people in. But, for those ads that actually "pull" in people and gain you business at the same time, you generally need to hire an advertising agency. The Yellow Pages advertisements usually only attract one-time clients who are frugal with their funds. It is for this reason that we normally do not recommend any Yellow Pages ads for most of the higher-priced service ads.

Advertising works with other branding channels by: directing people to your Web site when you publish your Web site address, promoting an upcoming seminar, making people aware of your business so that they are more receptive when you call on them, complementing any sponsorships you have, and they help to add credibility to your business, client referrals, and you in general by making you more visible.

Advertising can be more effectively used by: asking people to answer your ad in some specific way (like providing a special discount or asking those who see or hear your ad to call for a brochure), including your Web site address in all advertisements you put out, keeping your ads fresh at least every three months or so, making your ads more benefit-oriented by making them more about the customer and what they get from your services and not all about your business, and offering a great discount on your services when they mention that they heard about you from your ad.

Trade Shows and Special Events — Normally, a business should not even consider doing these larger-scale things until they have been in business, and been working hard at their professional branding, for at least a year. There are some exceptions to this rule, such as a very specific target market that spends most of their time shopping for your services at trade shows or special events, but generally, for service providers, leave these out for a while. This is because within your first year or so of business, you are still trying to refine your personal branding strategy and your marketing messages will still be in these stages as well. You will not be ready for the high demands and the chaos that trade shows have, or the extremely short attention spans that big crowds have at these shows or events. Also, the costs for these events are generally not worth it for a small business since you will have to provide for booths, shipping, giveaway items, accommodations, and transportation. It is an expensive branding channel.

Trade shows and special events are good for: networking, networking, and more networking. People that come to these types of events are there to make new contacts just as much as you are. They are also there to make buying decisions, and more. So, you need to know that your collection of business cards will grow by mountains after one of these large events, and it can be worth its weight in gold. Trade shows are great and powerful ways to step out of your local niche and gain access into a huge, national market with much more exposure. These shows are also great for making cool demonstrations of your products and services, complete with all the flash you can throw in.

Trade shows and special events are bad for: establishing any type of meaningful talks between you and a prospect. There is way too much going on at these events for any kind of conversation, and the majority of the people who attend these will come into your booth, take your free gifts and information, and then dump them when they get home (or before) and will not think about it again. So, if you consider the high cost of trade shows and other special events, there is not a significant return on your investment to make a big difference to a small company.

Trade shows and special events can work with other branding channels to: provide the press with a great media event to cover, give your business an extremely busy channel to distribute your business information and personal brochure, serve as a platform for upcoming speaking engagements and follow-up networking in the weeks that follow, build your database for direct mailings, and allow you to display your Web site address constantly.

Trade shows and special events can be used more effectively by: using recycled exhibit booths and other facilities, attending only those shows that focus on your target market, attending smaller events, having a great giveaway item that people will remember, have a video or DVD presentation or other visual aids to help sell your business to the crowd, and making sure that the return on your investment is worth it by gaining all the business cards possible during the show.

Exclusive Channels

Professional Referrals — These are some of the best possible ways to gain new clients and to get your branding information out there without a lot of cost. There is absolutely nothing better than a business referral. It is free, it is personal, and it has already come to you ready to purchase your services due to the credibility of the person who gave the referral in the first place. If you never do anything else to help promote your business or yourself, then you need to cultivate a great referral channel for your best clients to send people to you.

Professional referrals happen when another business, colleague, or other business friend recommends you to their customers or clients. These people will already have a higher degree of credibility with the referral, and when they recommend you to them, you are almost guaranteed to get a call or appointment. Think about it: if each of your associated professionals has hundreds of clients, and they send you some professional referrals, it can open a new doorway into all the VIP clients you can handle.

So, if these referrals are such free gold, why do more business professionals not use them? They think that most referrals just happen on their own. This could not be further from the truth. To gain a great referral base from professional contacts that you have, you have to ask for them. Make it an easy step for the person referring the potential clients to you and then develop a reward for them each time they do it. By providing something in return for the referrer, you will gain more referrals.

Professional referrals are good for: growing your new business sources without spending a lot of advertising dollars. Cultivating a referral base is all about picking the right people and building a great relationship with them. By knowing your professional referrers on a personal basis, you will gain a friendship that can benefit you both.

Professional referrals are bad for: not much. There is not a lot that is bad about professional referrals since they are free, the potential client comes to you already knowledgeable about you and your business, and they come ready to purchase your services. The only down side to professional referrals is that you cannot control what is said about you to the potential client.

Professional referrals can work with other branding channels by: setting up a great stage for a phone call or direct mail, preparing someone to get your information and personal brochure, directing more traffic to your Web site to learn about you and your business, and by making a potential client more receptive to your articles or PR work.

Professional referrals can be used more effectively by: identifying your associated professionals and speaking to them directly about setting up an informal arrangement to refer clients to each other, making sure the first target of your personal branding is your pool of associated professionals (if they do not know what your brand is about, they cannot refer the right people to you), making sure your referral pool has plenty of copies of your personal brochure or any other informative materials to give out, asking for the referrals by putting your referral pool on a regular direct mail basis to remind them about what you can do to help them and you, practicing quid pro quo and being sure to reward those who send you referrals, setting up incentive programs for those who send referrals to you (but making sure you check into the legality of this as some professions do not allow this and it is illegal in those areas), and most of all, treating any referral that walks through your door like gold. You should treat referrals better than you would normal clients off the street because that is the way that you continue to gain referrals.

Personal Referrals — There are no ads, brochures, literature, or Web sites that can get your foot in the door faster with new clients than by referrals. If a good report is given from someone who is used to you and who thinks you are great at what you do, that is all the endorsement you will ever need to get great referrals. If you make sure your clients are all completely happy, then it is time to use that and turn them into a great referral source.

Personal referrals are good for: getting out the word that you are good at what you do. This means the people who are talking about you are building up your skills and abilities to others and telling them how great you are. Nothing will help to build your personal brand faster than a good report from someone who likes you, trusts you, and wants everyone to know that. They will help other people they know and trust to get their services from you and this is a valuable resource. There are some businesses who gain all of their new clients from referrals because they have built their businesses so well; their clients are completely happy with them and cannot wait to tell other people about it.

Personal referrals are bad for: predictability. You cannot control what other people say about you, and you cannot make them say anything, either good or bad. So, until you have a constant flow of information going on through your happy clientele, you will not be able to rely on this route of gaining new customers.

Personal referrals can work with other branding channels by: preparing people for your calls; sending prospects to your Web site to learn about you and your business before they visit with you personally; getting them to call for information about you, your business, or an upcoming seminar, or to request one of your personal brochures; and it is great for setting the stage for networking opportunities.

Personal referrals can be used more effectively by: asking for referrals (few business owners actually ask for the referrals, so they do not ever get them), giving your clients extra materials to give out to friends and family members, creating a reward program for your clients who send people to you that purchase your services, and establishing a customer service program that will help to ensure those clients who are referred are treated like royalty in your office.

Direct Mail — Direct mail is probably the most strategically important branding channel for developing your personal brand. This is because it allows you to customize your message to each prospect who reads your information, sees your ad, or hears your commercials. Direct mail can be done in so many different ways, such as: letters, personal postcards, personal brochures, dimensional mailers, and more. Colored information is always better than plain black and white because not only are they cost effective, but they are easier to read and there is a better chance that your prospect will read it.

Direct mail is good for: putting your brand and information directly in front of many different prospects each month. Any type of consistent direct mail campaign can be one of the best ways to continually generate a new flow of business each and every month. It is also great for starting a relationship with potential clients, sending out news about new items or services you offer and more, sending out holiday greetings, and inviting these clients and their friends to open houses or for special discounts.

Direct mail is bad for: businesses who do not have a large advertising budget or who have fickle customers. This type of branding channel only works if you have the budget to send out good-quality information constantly. So if you are not willing to, or you cannot make the investment in the advertising literature, then it is not worth starting it. As for fickle customers, some people cannot stand any type of direct mail, and will not read anything you send.

Direct mail can work with other branding channels by: promoting seminars and other special events you are hosting, informing people about articles or columns that you are doing, asking for referrals, and informing readers about any new material on your Web site.

Direct mail can be used more effectively by: mailing more consistently, offering your prospective clients a great benefit (like a free service or great discount if they mention your mailer), making sure you have your phone number and Web site address on the information that is sent out, knowing your target market and designing the messages so that they appeal to them, and spending the money to make sure you send out great mailers — do not send out black-and-white junk that is hard to read. Send out something beautifully colored and attractive.

Networking — This involves making contacts with both colleagues and potential clients. Normally, people network everywhere, but this is most often done at larger events such as: public gatherings, trade shows, and seminars. The main goal of networking is to get people familiar with your name and your business, which lays the ground work for great business and personal relationships so you can hand out materials those people will keep.

Networking is good for: Letting those key players in your profession, community, and target market know about you and your business. Once you get those contacts, you can start to give them more personal information about you and your business, such as your personal brochure, to get them to know you better and to trust you. It is more than common knowledge that people will do business with people that they like, so networking can be a gold mine if you do it right.

Networking is bad for: gaining immediate business. While networking can be a great way to gain some quick friends and influential contacts, it is not always a great way to earn business right away and make money. In fact, if you use your networking time to try to push people to buy right away, you will find that your networking will become a disaster. People do not want to be hounded and treated as resources for your business, so the best way to gain their trust and business is to become their friend first.

Networking can work with other branding channels by: generating referrals, allowing you to give out your personal brochure and business information, and giving you the opportunity to tell people about your seminars, articles, columns, and other publications.

Networking can be used more effectively by: joining professional organizations where you can meet more people who work in your field or with your target market, focusing on creating relationships with professionals who have clients in your target market or clients who may need your services as well (these are great ways to gain referrals), keeping personal brochures on you at all times to hand out when you are networking, avoiding selling your business or services to people you are networking with (simply talking with people and having a great time is the best way to network), and having a great follow-up plan in motion for contacting people after the event to help drive home your name and friendship to them.

Warm Calling — Cold calling is swiftly becoming a waste of time. "Warm calling" is where you contact people that you have already talked to before. These are people that you have already met through your seminars, networking, referrals, or other methods. Warm calling is the kind of telemarketing that gives you a way to further your relationship with that person by offering them more information about you and your business, and offering your services to them.

Warm calling is good for: taking your relationship with a contact to the next level by cementing in your name and business. It is also good for setting up a meeting with the person to get face-to-face once more, and allow them to get to know you on a more personal level. By talking to these contacts, answering their questions, and earning their trust by showing them your knowledge, you will gain their business.

Warm calling is bad for: business owners who already have busy schedules. Telemarketing is the exact opposite of advertising in the sense that it is very time consuming. So, you will have to set aside large chunks of your time to make warm calls to contacts and take the time to speak with all of them directly to gain their business. It is not a good idea to have other people make these calls for you, as they then turn into cold calls.

Warm calling can work with other branding channels by: capitalizing on referrals, letting you invite people to seminars or events personally, and asking them to send a referral to you or add people to your mailing list.

Warm calling can be used more effectively by: only calling people who have come into contact with you personally, always having a great benefit to share with them if they listen to your pitch, talking to them and not trying to sell them right then, and making sure to ask if they know anyone who can use your services. If someone asks to be taken off your list, do it right away. Finally, if the call is successful, send them out a thank-you card immediately before they come in for their appointment.

How to Make the Most of Your Branding Channels

Now that you know the basics of branding channels and how to push your business out into other areas and markets, there are a few more tips that I can give you to ensure that you are doing everything possible to gain the most from your marketing. Here are four tips that you should live by in your business:

1. Always cross-promote your business. Put your Web site address on all your business information, press releases, and advertising. Refer to your advertising in your direct mailings, Web site, and hand out seminar invitations when you are networking. Constantly be thinking up ways to let your branding channels overlap.

2. Do not overcommit yourself. The five channels presented in this book are optional. While they make for an optimal strategy, you do not have to use all five. Sometimes just networking, a great Web site, and direct mail are all you need to get the word out about your business.

3. Constantly update and build your database. When you contact anyone, try to get all the contact information that you can. It does not matter if they are a contact, potential client, or corporate executive — keep their information handy and in a big database.

4. Make sure your base information (such as your business name and logo) is always visible in anything that you do.

As with anything in business, there are dos and don'ts that you should follow. I have given you the dos, so here are the don'ts that you should avoid at all costs:

1. Do not starve your branding channels out. Once you open one channel, keep it open for branding and marketing information by keeping your information going through it constantly.

2. The most expensive branding channels are not always the right ones for all businesses. So do not allow yourself to be seduced by the dollars that it costs.

3. Do not adopt someone else's branding channel strictly out of envy. If you see one of your competitor's ads on a flashy television commercial, resist the urge to run out and spend thousands of dollars on one for your company. Stick with the target branding channels that you have already set up and that have worked for you.

4. Do not worry about the cost if the branding channel is getting you great results. If one channel is costing you $10,000 per year but it brings in $60,000 per year, then it is worth the money.

5. Do not abandon a branding channel before a six-month time limit. Some channels take time to get your message saturated enough that people take notice. So keep a branding channel around for six months before you abandon it or you will lose your investment.

6. If you have trouble in one channel — such as speaking in front of a large crowd and it completely flops — isolate that one channel from the others until you learn where the problem was. You do not want that problem to bleed over into other branding channels that are working well for you.

This chapter should have you contemplating all the different branding channels that you can utilize for your business to help it spread out and grow. Use this chapter as a constant guide on where to put your focus and advertising dollars when it comes to branding channels, and you will always have a great list when you need to add new channels or switch. The next chapter will show you how to make your business visible to all by using some of these same branding channels.

Chapter 6: Learn to Make Your Business Visible to All

For those just starting out in the business world, make sure your business is visible to everyone possible so you can start to pull in those VIP clients that you desire. For those who have an established business, making sure that your business is visible to all only helps increase the VIP clients that you will bring in as well. But keeping your business visible to everyone is not quite as easy as it sounds. You cannot simply put out a sign, create a Web site, or do a radio commercial and assume that you have done everything to make your business visible to all. While it is not an impossible job, it is a bit hard at first to get into the habit of making your business always visible. Once you get the hang of it, you will find that it becomes second nature.

Is your business visible to all? How can you tell? Well, ask yourself the following questions to see how visible your business is to everyone out there:

1. When was the last time that your name, or business name, appeared in print?

2. When was the last time that you changed your advertising strategies?

3. Are you being contacted by new clients at least once a day?

4. Does the local press contact you for expert information or advice?

5. Do you advertise on local venues as well as online and in other venues?

If you answered no to any of these questions, then there is more you can do to make sure your business is visible to everyone that it possibly can be.

One of the main keys to succeeding in business is to have your branding message out there constantly, so that it keeps your name on potential client's minds. This is the true meaning of visibility, and if you cannot stay visible to potential clients, then your business will fail. If you have not done any type of marketing in months, then you are missing getting clients because they are forgetting about you and your business, so they are calling your competition. Remember that your competition is not forgetting to market themselves or their businesses, and they are fresh in potential clients' minds.

Keeping a high level of visibility is the cornerstone of every successful business strategy and it begins with placing your branding message in front of as many people in your target market as you possibly can, as often as you possibly can.

We have already explored several different ways to keep your business and yourself visible to potential clients, and we will learn more ways in other chapters. The key is to find the right mix of marketing materials and avenues so that you have a constant flow of yourself and your business in front of your potential clients. Different types of businesses will find that certain types of marketing will work great while others do not.

One of the first things you should do to begin making your business visible to all is to pay attention to the types of marketing that your competition is doing and ask yourself why they are using that particular way of marketing their business. For example, if they are using several different radio ads, consider why they have gone with that type of marketing instead of print advertisements. Or, if they are using large billboards around your area, think about what the potential is for getting to their target market with them. By evaluating your competition's marketing strategies, you will find better ways to create your own that will work more in your favor and less in theirs.

Once you have a pretty good grasp on what your competition is doing to market themselves and their business, you can then start to make a list of the different types of marketing that you want to try for your business. Feel free with this first list to put down every type of marketing that you want to do, no matter if you think you have the money for it or not. If you think it will be a good marketing tactic for your business, write it down.

Now take a good look at your list. Start with the first one you wrote down and slowly go down the list, evaluating each different marketing tactic. Consider the cost of that tactic, the potential for client feedback, how many people your message will reach with that particular marketing ploy, and so on. When you find something that will not work for your business, such as a large cost for the marketing tactic, then cross it off. Go through your list thoroughly until you have about three or four good, solid marketing tactics that you feel you can do that will truly help your business grow and succeed.

When you have a short list of marketing tactics that will fit with your business well and can be done each month, then you are ready to start making your business visible to all your potential clients. Start by implementing the easiest of the marketing tactics on your list first. Make sure you have the ability to do it, or hire a professional to do it for you; this way, potential clients will not think you are a fly-by-night business. Once you have your first marketing tactic in motion, move on to the next one in a few days or so. You want to make sure that you can put a new marketing tactic into motion at the rate of one per week for a month when you start marketing your business. By saturating the market right away with marketing tactics that you have chosen, you will either see an increase in calls and potential clients right away, or you will see that these are not the right tactics for your business. Either way, you will be getting your brand and message in front of potential clients right away, and making sure that there are several avenues to showing off your message to those potential clients.

Once you learn which tactics work, and which do not, you can refine your marketing to target the right potential clients. When you have chosen a marketing strategy, then you can set it into motion so that it continues to work each month to bring in new clients and new prospects. You must remember to keep the marketing rolling each month, and do not let any month go by that you do not market your business in some way to potential clients. By keeping your business name, brand, marketing message, or any other part of your business in front of them, your business will automatically be in the front of their mind when they need your services.

In the next chapter, we will show you how to make your business stand out from your competition so that your marketing tactics will not just prod your prospective clients to call just anyone — only you.

Chapter 7: Make Your Business Stand Out From the Rest

In today's highly competitive business market, you must constantly find ways to make your business stand out from your competition. This means you have to come up with a strategy that makes your business completely unique from the others by showing your target market the value that you can deliver to them that is above the rest.

Some businesses happen on their unique positioning strategy by accident, and some must sit and think about it before they can come up with one that they can use. But any business has to begin by developing a unique positioning strategy that will help to position the business way above the others. This will distinguish your brand in the market with one simple message that will communicate the value that you deliver to the client. If you cannot do this, your target market will simply think of you as another business out there, offering the same thing as someone else.

Your target market position should come from the main characteristics of your product or service. The elements that can go into your unique position can include:

1. Is the quality you offer better than the rest? Is the product or service that you offer very well put together or produced? What type of quality control standards do you have in place? What are the national or international standards that you have to meet? Do you offer warranties, guarantees, or claims that back up your product or service?

2. What other benefits do you offer your clients? What do those customers who choose your business get when they use you? Do they get increased comfort? Do they become financially stable? Do they get an increase in their business? This should be one of the key areas of your positioning strategy.

3. Is your price different from the competition's? Is the product or service you offer a luxury service, a middle-of-the-road service, or on the cheaper end? Pricing is an effective way of making yourself stand out from others in your field.

4. Does your business offer special services? All customers and clients will expect good service, but do you offer something different or special? Do you offer Web-based customer service or a toll-free number that clients can call? Do you have a special guarantee? Is your product or service customized or personalized? Do you offer a faster turnaround than your competition?

If your business is surrounded by businesses who offer the same things that you do, then you need to combine these different elements to ensure that you have a better value to your target market than the business down the road. By creating a unique positioning strategy, you can make your business stand out above the rest.

You should start by doing research so you can understand the current prices in your specific market, the current practices, the practices that your competitors offer, and which practices you will want to adopt, or not, to help you achieve your goals.

Here are some questions that you should ask yourself:

1. Can you save your clients money?
2. Can you save your clients time?
3. Can you make money for people?
4. Can you offer a larger selection than your competition?
5. Is your office conveniently located compared to your competition?
6. Can you give free installations, initial consultations, inspections, or other promotional services?
7. Are your prices better than the competition's?
8. Can you offer a faster turnaround on your services?
9. Can you guarantee that you offer the lowest price?
10. Will you meet or beat the competition's pricing?
11. Will you honor any special discounts that your competition offers customers?
12. Can you give a stronger guarantee than the competition?
13. Does your office use technology that is faster and more reliable?

While you do not have to be extremely original in every bit of your business, you should still offer something that is significantly different than your competition and that is superior to what they offer.

Remember that "positioning is power." Your position in the market creates a strong bond between your business and a potential client's or customer's mind. Once you have established this bond, your business's name will pop into your clients' heads automatically when they need your services or products. The most important thing to remember is that the positioning of your business is not based on what you do to a service or product; it is what you do to the minds of your potential clients.

Develop Your Positioning Statement

Your positioning statement is your special promise to your clients and your target market that communicates how you will provide them with the benefits that matter the most to them. The trick to this is to capture the special promise in an extremely short phrase and make that phrase very compelling.

Imagine this: You are in an elevator with someone who is a potential client. She begins to talk to you, and you only have about 30 seconds to answer her question, "What do you do?" Well, your positioning statement should answer this question in just a couple of sentences or less, clearly stating the benefits that you offer clients, and why they should choose you. Your positioning statement will define what is important to your business and what makes it appealing to your clients.

Here are a few examples of positioning statements:

- Our design firm specializes in refurbishing Art Deco homes.

- Our accounting firm specializes in nonprofit organizations in the Los Angeles area.

- We offer an all-organic, Mexican grocery market.

- Our consulting firm helps professional services attract more clients.

If you keep your positioning statement short and easy to remember, but still focused on your business, then you will never forget it. If you cannot explain your positioning statement in one or two sentences, you will have a hard time getting that potential client in the elevator to remember your name or business after you have left.

How to Find Your Market Niche

Since the business marketplace is constantly evolving and changing, you will have to learn to be completely plugged in to the latest information. This will help you stay on top of major changes in your field and help to keep your business competitive.

You should always approach market research with an open mind and a strong willingness to make changes in your business or the direction it takes if necessary. Keep in mind that market research can show you that your target market niche is not predisposed to purchasing your service, or that they are already overwhelmed with businesses that already offer them.

Remember that the hardest part about market research is not

finding the data or understanding it — it is that market research can burst your bubble when it comes to your target market.

By using your market research correctly, you can easily change what you feel your target market is. How do you know what your target market is, or should be? We will explore that in our next chapter.

Chapter 8: Finding Your Target Market

Most business owners think they need to dominate every single market out there to become a complete success. But this simply is not true. For a small business, simply learning to dominate one specific market is more than enough to keep a business going and growing for years to come. With an attitude that you only need to dominate your target market, you will find that your marketing will swiftly become almost effortless.

You will probably hear the term "market niche" when it comes to your target market. A target market and market niche is essentially the same thing, and you can choose either term you are more comfortable with. We will go with target market for this book, since this is all about marketing to that target market to help your business grow and prosper.

You can define your target market by many different factors: region, customer needs, demographics, age group, and so on. But no matter how you define your target market, you will need to do some research and know exactly who you are marketing to before you begin any type of marketing campaign.

The business owners who know exactly who their target market is seem to attract tons of clients with little or no effort. It seems they simply wave their hand and people come running. It seems they do not make any cold calls, or they do not spend any money on advertising, but they still are constantly in the paper or magazines, they are always speaking at conferences, and everyone knows who they are and what they do. The business just falls into their laps, and it is as if they are completely famous in their area.

Actually, this is close to the truth. They are a bit famous, but not in the same way that we think of movie stars or athletes. They are simply famous enough that their name comes to mind when people are looking for something special that they offer, such as their services or products. They use this fame to reap the benefits of their business, by gaining more business and the right kind of business.

Every business owner wants to have this and enjoy this success, but it seems that few really achieve it. You want it? Well, have no fear — that is why you are reading this book! Just keep in mind that it may require you to change your way of thinking and develop new marketing strategies that you would not have thought of before. And even though, to someone looking in, it may seem like you are not putting in any effort, it will require work from you.

Becoming Just a Little Bit Famous

In a crowded business market, your potential clients have a ton of choices, so you have to stand out by being just a little bit famous. This is the opposite of mass marketing. It is not about being everything to everyone, but instead about being just a little bit famous to the right group of people. It is all about finding your target market and developing your reputation with them as a great resource for their needs. You need to be knowledgeable, trustworthy, and close.

Your goal will be to become the lord of your domain, which will be a smaller, profitable domain of your choosing. In this domain, you will be able to attract more customers and clients, sorting out your VIP clients in the process.

Of course, these type of results will require a very thought-out and constant effort. The effort that you will need to put into this domain will come in many different forms, but underneath it all, you will find six basic principles:

1. Target the right prospects to create your domain

2. Develop a special market niche to market your services

3. Position your business as the best in your field for your target market

4. Maintain the highest visibility for your business

5. Enhance your business's credibility — and yours — with your target market

6. Establish your brand and its reputation in your target market

By refining these principles, you will be able to create a recipe for success that will help you pull your business out of that anonymity trap that so many of your competitors will be caught in. This will also help to create just a little bit of fame for you and your business, which will build a successful business. In the next section, we will take a more in-depth look at how you should use these principles and what you need to do to put each one into action.

Targeting the Right Prospects to Create Your Domain

This is where market research comes in. Market research is like testing the temperature of the pool before you jump in. It should help you know who you are marketing your business or services to, what their needs are, and help you avoid wasting time with costly advertising campaigns and poor marketing promotions. You can change your services or products to fit your target market, and you can also craft your business's message so that it reflects your customers. Market research should not have to involve expensive consultants, groups, polls, or surveys — it can be as easy as asking your best customers the right questions that will help you learn what they need, and what they like about your business the best.

It is not hard to find your target market. Take a look at your best customers. Make a short list of what is similar about them. For example, are they all seniors? Are they all looking for the same types of services? Do they all respect your business because of your expertise? There are many different factors that can go into determining your target market. If you cannot think of the things that make your best customers similar, give your best customers a poll with some simple questions about what they like best about your business or services or ask them to rate your business or services. Their answers will give you a clear picture of what they are all looking for when it comes to services that you provide, and you should get a clear picture of who your target market it.

You do not have to be a member of your target market either. For example, you can be in your 30s and still market to a senior target market. As long as you talk to enough people in that market, you should have a feeling as to what they want and need. You will have to be aware of their concerns, needs, and wants, and constantly keep an ear out for more information.

Once you have talked to enough people within your target market, you will learn the best marketing techniques and tactics that they respond to. Now that you know what your target market is, and how to market to them, you will be able to become just a little bit famous in your area of business.

Developing a Special Market Niche to Market Your Services

Since most of the larger companies will be out to dominate the global marketplace, and not focusing their efforts on their target market, this leaves the door wide open for you to market your services to a specific group. When you use your skills and market research to determine your special market niche, you will also be able to refine your marketing skills so that you bring in a constant stream of new clients and still keep those VIP clients you have already gained.

Your business's special market niche can be defined by using many different factors. Some of these factors we already learned about, such as age, demographics, needs, and region. Or a special market niche can be determined by a special product that is a simple variation on an older, established one.

There are so many different ways that you can find a special market niche to market your services to, the trick is to choose just one or two, once you have a massive list. Once you choose the right special market niche, you will find that your marketing will become easier, and it will appear to those on the outside that you are not doing a thing.

Position Your Business as the Best in Your Field for Your Target Market

In an overcrowded market, it is no longer enough to carve out your special niche. You may have narrowed your focus group down into your target market, but you will still have competition. Now is the time to distinguish your business, and yourself, as the preeminent source of service and solutions for your target market, by refining your expertise and conveying this expertise to your market. You should know more than your competition about something, or be better than them at something, and you have to market this skill and let everyone know.

Once you can honestly convey such a message to your target market, the potential customers and clients will see this, and start to see you and your business as the obvious answer to their needs. You will then become their logical choice when they are looking for services that you provide.

Maintain the Highest Visibility for Your Business

Think back to the last time that your name, or business name, was in print. Yesterday? A month ago? Years ago? Even if you can think of the last time that your name was in print, it does not mean that your customers will.

One of the major keys to success in your target marketplace is to have your business's message out there, almost continually. It should be kept out there so often that it keeps your name alive in your customers' minds. This is what visibility means, and if you are not visible to your potential customers, then someone else will be, and you will cease to exist.

If you have not done any marketing in several months, then you are missing getting clients because they are forgetting who you are. This means they are calling your competition, and not you, for the same services that you provide, since they are keeping themselves visible to everyone.

Visibility should be one of the major foundation stones of making your business become a little bit famous. This strategy begins by placing your core marketing message in front of as many people in your target market as possible, as often as possible, and as long as possible.

Enhance Your Business's Credibility With Your Target Market

Of course, visibility is only a means of getting your business in front of people. To produce the results that you want, visibility has to be combined with credibility. This means you have to learn to embrace the strategies that will convey how distinct your business is, by making visible your competence, authority, leadership, and expertise in your field. This is what will help to make you a little bit famous, and go far beyond the simple marketing strategies that your competition will use. Networking expert Bob Burg explains positioning your business like this: "The key is to position yourself in your market as the expert, the resource, the only person your prospect would ever even think of doing business with, or referring to others."

Becoming a "recognized" expert in your field is the fastest way to develop a very credible name for yourself. But who actually counts as an expert? Experts include the following: speakers, consultants, business owners, authors, professionals, and managers. If you have a wealth of in-depth knowledge on a specific subject, even if it is your business, then you qualify as an expert. The test of an expert is to determine how much you know, and if you know much about a subject, you can use that to leverage your knowledge into a wonderful halo of authority.

Once you have established yourself as an authority, you can then write articles for trade and special interest publications. If you are too busy to write, or you worry about your writing skills, then you can find help with this. You can use the Web or Yellow Pages for "editing" or "writing" services. You can do speaking engagements. Or, you can simply become a news resource, providing quotes to the media for issues that relate to your business or industry.

In addition to putting yourself in the news, you can also start to create information products, such as booklets, class guides, and audio cassettes that revolve around your expertise. These will help to firmly place you, and your business, as a leader in your market niche.

Establish Your Brand and Its Reputation in Your Target Market

You will swiftly find that nothing in the world will overcome consumer skepticism more quickly than a good report from someone who has used your services before. When people have a friend or family member recommend you, they will approach you with a more positive attitude and better expectations. In essence, they will already have an assurance that will take any of the risk out of doing business with you. So, if you can couple a good recommendation from a client with your name constantly in front of them, the effect of this great marketing strategy can grow at lightning speed.

Here is the formula that marketing guru Marcia Yudkin uses to define how your reputation is built:

Visibility + Credibility + Word of Mouth = **REPUTATION**

Remember that this equation is not possible unless you provide the great customer satisfaction that people will tell their friends and family about. There are tons of great titles on customer service on the market today, and it is always a great idea to read up on customer service so you can stay on top of your game when it comes to that area. Without great visibility, you can offer great customer service and excellent services to your clients, but you will still find yourself without enough business to stay open.

Yet if you pursue your visibility and credibility marketing strategies and still provide a great service or product, then word of mouth will take off on its own. Though you cannot be personally present for every moment when your potential clients are considering your services, your reputation will be set in place as a great surrogate salesperson in your potential client's mind.

Remember that large corporations will spend millions on promoting a special brand because it pays for them to do so. However, the best known brands will be spread at the speed of gossip, from one potential client to another — town to town, state to state. You are probably not in the position to spend millions on a brand campaign, but there are plenty of economical ways that you can make your business just as attractive as those huge corporations with a distinguishable microbrand that conveys your values and expertise.

The brand that you create will integrate all of your marketing around one core idea and vision. This will also make it easier to know what to do to successfully market yourself and your business. Since you have a unique identity, you will have much less to worry about from your competition, and it will automatically open the door for new partnerships and business.

Once you have mastered these six basic principles for success, you will find that marketing and advertising will come easier to you all the time, and will free you up to concentrate on your business and your services. It will also ensure that your marketing efforts pull in the VIP clients that you fought to determine from your current business. So there will be less wasted time on that front as well, opening the door for clients that fit your VIP profile. This strategy will help to make you, and your business, a little bit famous — enough to let you stand out in your market and allow you all the business you need.

CASE STUDY: ANDREW RONDEAU

Great Management
UK
http://www.greatmanagement.org
andrew@greatmanagement.org
(+44) 790 099 5932
Andrew Rondeau — Creator and Owner

I have worked as a Manager in the corporate world for the last 25 years. My experience covers such industries as retail, IT, manufacturing, and financial, but all my life I have worked for someone else and I wanted to see if I could make it on my own. I had a very successful career as a manager, managing teams of up to 1000 people and that was it, I was going to share my experience. I was going to become a millionaire! How wrong was I?

I created **http://www.greatmanagement.org**, a Web site offering free information on how to improve your career and management skills. Obviously I needed some income too, so I also created my own management-related and career-related products, and now I needed to market both them and the Web site.

CASE STUDY: ANDREW RONDEAU

I did the "normal" things and still do today. Writing press releases and articles to distribute across the Internet, contribute on forums, blogging; all the normal stuff everyone is doing and all this was attracting visitors to my Web site and sales of my products were adequate. However, the sales had only covered a small amount of what I had spent on the set-up and the effort I had put into the new adventure. This was not good, so I had to think of another way.

I therefore decided to study the individuals in bookshops. Look at what management books were being purchased and why did they buy those ones? Some purchasers said they bought the books because they liked the cover, or they liked the write-up, but the majority said, "Because I have heard of the author and he/she is respected," some even saying "I buy all of his/her books."

So that was the secret. Become world-famous and then sell your products! I had no chance — an unknown like me getting his products sold. They are just as good as theirs, if not better as I had 25 successful years as a manager and knew how to manage.

I thought, "Why not build relationships with these famous authors," maybe get them to talk to me, or give me their opinion on my products; that must help. So I wrote to them and phoned their offices, asking to interview them and then using the interview on my Web site. Many said, "No; don't have time." However, lots of them said "yes" right away. I have kept a list of those of who said "yes," because when I am just as famous, I would like to be there when those individuals want me to help them.

By getting those interviews and building up those relationships, it made my Web site credible. It has made a tremendous difference to my visitors and sales, with my visitor numbers increasing tenfold and my conversion rate improving 100 percent.

The next stage, of course, is to get the famous authors to endorse my products. But that will be in the next book!

Part Two

Start Your Business's Engine

Chapter 9: Create a Unique Positioning Statement for Your Business
Chapter 10: Building Your Business's Credibility
Chapter 11: Networking Is Key
Chapter 12: Forming Alliances With Vendors
Chapter 13: Learn the Art of the Article
Chapter 14: Learn to Use the Media to Your Advantage
Chapter 15: Some Pitfalls to Avoid

Now that you have some of the basic pillars laid for your business's foundation, it is time to start up the main engine that will crank your business into high gear. After the leg work is done with the set-up and creation of a logo and the basic view of your business, it is time to focus your efforts on other areas that can help to build up your business fast.

This part of the book will focus on helping you refine the things that you set into motion in the first part of this book, such as your positioning statement, building credibility, and using the media to your advantage. There are so many different ways that you can develop your business's image, and we will cover several of them here, but remember that these are not the only ways that you can do this. By keeping a creative mind always open and thinking, you will be able to take the information from this book and create a wonderfully unique business statement, visibility strategy, media strategy, and more to help your business grow and succeed.

There are so many different areas that are covered in this part of the book that will deal with how your business is viewed by other people, such as clients, business contacts, vendors, and the public. I will take you through the steps that will help you use the media to increase your business's visibility and to help you become a local celebrity and expert in your field of business. I will also take you through the steps to powerful networking so you can make the most of any networking time you have with other business professionals, your potential target market, and the public.

While there are many different steps to making your business a success, remember that by keeping yourself motivated and your business running smoothly you will gain that success in any advertising endeavor that you try. Keep all of the information in this area of the book close to your brain while you are starting up the main engine of your business; in this way you will have a clear mind on what to do next when you finish each step.

Chapter 9: Create a Unique Positioning Statement for Your Business

Setting the Stage

You have established your personal brand and you have created a great marketing campaign around it. You have started up your networking and started the process of becoming known as an expert in your area. Now it is time to move on to the next level of getting clients through your doors.

When you created your brand, the purpose behind it was to tell people how they should feel about your business and you. By doing that effectively, the message that you convey should not be complicated or confusing to anyone who comes across it. Remember that you are not trying to sell your life story to someone in less than ten seconds. As we learned earlier, if you keep your brand simple and clear, you can build on it with a positioning statement.

To keep your brand simple, make sure you follow these three steps:

1. Tell who you are
2. Tell what you do

3. Tell what makes you different and how you bring great value to the customer

Tell who you are. Most larger companies forget this first step. People do not know, and usually do not care, who you are until you give them a reason to. This is the main goal of your personal brand and one of the foundations for your positioning statement. Always keep it simple enough that people will remember, but keep enough flair in it to be different than all the others.

Tell what you do. You would be surprised at the number of companies that skip this step. Most businesses assume people automatically can read their minds without being told what the business actually does. But there is a trick to this. You cannot simply say that you are an attorney, for example. There are thousands of attorneys all over the world. You need to find a way to tell people that you are a family attorney without being so simple.

Tell what makes you different and how you bring great value to the customer. You have to separate yourself from all those other attorneys by taking a good look at what really makes you different from the others and then letting your target market know this, such as focusing on family cases and providing a cheaper rate for lower-income families. When you know what makes you different and special, you can place a marketing spin on it to gain a better grip on your target market.

Creating a Unique Positioning Statement for Your Business

Now that you have the three core elements of your brand in place, you can begin to work on your positioning statement.

CHAPTER 9: CREATE A UNIQUE POSITIONING STATEMENT FOR YOUR BUSINESS

This involves taking those three elements and putting them all together into one simple sentence that sums it up.

For example, take a Realtor who specializes in properties that need to be fixed up. After he creates his three elements, he can then take them and put them all into one unique positioning statement, which could read something like this:

"A New York native finding buyers those great specialty homes with a high value and low price and helping buyers manage the tax aspects of their property to the benefit of all parties."

Notice that it does not say anywhere that he is a real estate agent, because the positioning statement is clear enough that it conveys this message right away. It does not take a lot of editing to create a great positioning statement that is clear and easy to read and still conveys your message to anyone who reads it. In a few short words, he has told anyone who reads his positioning statement everything they need to know about what he does to determine if he is the right person to provide the services they need.

Once you have your three elements in place, sit down and practice writing your positioning statement until you find one that flows well and conveys everything you want it to. Do not worry if it takes you several tries before you get it right; sometimes the elements do not fit together at first. Keep editing and changing things around until you have a positioning statement that will define exactly what you want it to.

Chapter 10: Building Your Business's Credibility

So, we have gone through the whole process of creating your personal brand, positioning yourself as an expert in your field, making your business visible, and even how to create awesome logos and branding materials. Now you need to know how to build your business's credibility with potential clients and your peers. What you need to begin with are the "standard" credibility builders that will help to give you a base to build from. These are the basic things that every business needs to have in place to appear credible and professional to clients and the whole world. Once you have these basics covered and in place, then you can start to build more on your reputation as a major authority in your business area.

Here are six standard credibility builders that every business should have:

1. Have a professional email address. For example, bigbusinessman@yahoo.com does not work for a professional email address. Your email address for your business should come from your domain name, such as johndoe@doelawfirm.com. This is a professional email address. If you do not have a domain name yet, get one.

2. Spend the extra money on high-quality business cards. The cards that you can print yourself at home are not professional. The free printing cards that you can get with the printing company's name on the back are not professional. Take the extra time and money and design a professional business card that will be printed on a glossy card stock and will look professional. Cheap cards will only make your business look cheap.

3. Have a professional design your Web site. Sure, there are great site builders that will get you a basic site going, but unless you are a professional Web designer, do not do it yourself. Spend the money to have a professional Web site done.

4. Have professional photographs taken. You will need photos of yourself for your Web site, marketing materials, and many other things. If you use some picture that your mom took, it will not look professional, unless she is a professional photographer! Spend the extra money to have a couple of professional photos taken.

5. Gather and showcase specific testimonials about your services. If you only get general testimonials, like "John Doe was great to work with," it will not add a lot of credibility to you or your business. But specific testimonials are best, such as, "John Doe helped clear up our tax problems in a very professional manner. He not only helped us to create a better business budget, but he also helped us find several tax deductions that we did not even know we could use." This is a specific testimonial about a tax service and what they did to help the client. These are the types of testimonials that you need to showcase on your

site and other marketing materials that will give you better credibility with anyone who sees them.

6. Establish an "advisory board." If you know or can get some well-known names to lend you the use of their names, it will help tremendously in creating credibility within that target market you want to reach. Just associating with recognized experts will help build up your credibility.

These six simple steps will help you build up your business's credibility tremendously in a short amount of time. By showcasing these few things, your business will look, and feel, like a professional business instead of just another competitor on a list. If you and your business appear trustworthy, you will gain more clients than others.

By building your credibility, you will be able to hold more productive conversations when you begin to network for your business. The next chapter will present some of the main areas that you should network to build your business contacts and how you should view your networking to help you, and your business, grow.

Chapter 11: Networking Is Key

We have already learned about networking in previous chapters, but now we will dive into the world of networking further. As a business owner, you have to take a personal interest in networking and marketing to make your business successful. By making personal contacts, you will start to build a group of friends and business contacts who know and trust you, and will begin to send you referrals based on this trust.

Why Should I Network?

Let us start with the first question that comes to mind: Why should I network? Networking is a continually changing strategy that you will do throughout your business's life. It keeps you visible to those in the business world, and helps to firm relationships you have made along the way. It also means you will be the first to come to mind when those people need your services or know someone who does. Remember that there is no substitute for human contact. A little friendship and a handshake will go a long way in making friends and business contacts to further your business and personal life. The more that you network, the more distinctive you will make yourself and your business, and the more people will remember you and your business when they need you.

Networking is a constantly evolving strategy that will help you gain and maintain contacts to help your business grow. It is not something that you only do once, and it is not something that you can do for a little while and then stop. It is a constantly changing process that you should always be thinking about. It keeps your business visible to all, it helps to solidify your relationships with your contacts and friends, and it helps to ensure you come to people's minds when they, or people that they know, need something you offer.

Although there are myriad ways that you can communicate with people today, a little old-fashioned human contact is always best. This way, you are more distinctive than just Joe Schmo who sends an occasional email or makes a weekly phone call. You are in their office, taking them to lunch, chatting about life and business, and they feel that you truly care about them since you took the time to come see them personally. The more distinctive you make yourself and your business, the better you will be remembered when the time comes.

Make a Good Reputation for Yourself

Networking and building a good reputation go hand-in-hand. It does not matter where you are, what you are doing, or how you feel, you should always handle yourself in a professional and friendly manner so that people will see you as a professional business person. When you speak at a conference, discuss your business at a professional organization meeting, or hold a charity event, you are building your reputation.

The more friendly you are, and the more that you are willing to help people learn about your industry and what you can do to help them, the better your reputation will become as a top expert in your field. When you begin to build your reputation, make sure you stick to it and keep your word. By providing people with a reliable, constant, go-to person for your area, you will build up a great business and personal reputation.

While networking is a vital part of your business, your reputation is equally important. Every second of your business day, you are establishing your business reputation — when you talk to potential clients, when you speak at public events, when you develop a new marketing campaign. No matter what you do, your business' reputation is growing. Keep in mind that everything you do will become part of your reputation, no matter if it is good or bad.

When you are trying to develop your business's reputation, you need to work at it, just like you need to work at networking. Make sure you keep promises you make, and do what you say you will. Keep your word to clients, potential clients, contacts, vendors, and anyone else that you deal with through your business and personal life. If you cannot make good on a commitment, then let the person know immediately. Just like in your personal life, you should be concerned with your reputation and mold it to how you want people to see your business.

Target Your Networking So It Produces Maximum Results

Before you head out to try and meet as many people as you possibly can, you should do some homework first. Create a networking strategy that will help to advance your business goals by putting your business and yourself in front of the people who are in touch with your target market. There are several ways of finding great areas to focus your networking on so that you gain the maximum results possible. Here are a few of the different groups that you can do a bit of homework on to provide the optimal results for your business networking:

General Business Organizations — There are thousands of general business organizations all over the world that you can join who are as happy to have your membership as you are to have found them. It is easy to find these organizations — you can visit your local library for a list of local groups, search the Internet for global organizations, talk to clients in your target market to find out which organizations they are members of, and check trade magazines and publications for organization advertisements.

When you have found a few that seem to represent your target market extremely well, then do a small bit of homework before you pay any fees. Go to a couple of local meetings, talk to people who are members of the organization, read their newsletters and information, and look for opportunities to become involved with them as much as you can that will showcase your abilities and talents to the other members. When you are positive that the organization is a good fit, become a member with them.

Associations — You can do a simple search on the Internet and find thousands of associations that match any interest, any industry, and pretty much any profession there is out there today. These groups of people will provide some of the best possible networking opportunities, since they are focused on a specific set of interests. If your business serves those interests or helps to solve a problem that is common in that area, then you have struck gold.

By using associations to network for members in your target market, you gain the opportunity to become one of the preferred vendors for those members. This means you gain their business simply because you are in their association and they know you. This vendor strategy works great for areas that you have little or no competition in, so be creative in associations that you join.

Chambers of Commerce — Your local Chamber of Commerce can be a great way to network. Chambers usually have several different types of great networking opportunities, such as lead groups, meetings, seminars, and luncheons, all with members of different areas of the business community.

Just like with other groups, a membership with your Chamber of Commerce can be beneficial, but they work best when you truly get involved with the organization. When you go beyond the popular networking opportunities and "mixers," you will be able to gain a special recognition that people will instantly associate with you and your business. Any special leadership titles or groups that you can lead for the Chamber will promote your business and your reputation, and help you stand out.

Lead Groups — There are many great organizations that offer nothing but networking opportunities. These lead groups try to help reduce the industry overlap within the group by limiting the number of members in any certain field. Before you take the time and money it takes to join a lead group, talk to the members, and get a feel for the group and the tone of the group. Do they seem to be supportive of each other? Does the leadership of the group help support this as well? Or does it seem they are not receptive to new members or to new fields? By getting a feel for the group before you join, you will be able to find out if you will fit in and if the membership will be worth it or not.

Volunteering — One more excellent networking strategy is to volunteer your time with any organization or cause that allows you to meet many people. Most people do not think volunteer work will help you to network and to meet all sorts of people who might need your services. But the trick is to go for a cause that will be close to your heart and that you care about. In this way you will not come across as phony or as just another business person there to sell. If you find a cause that you are passionate about, then you will find that people will automatically associate that passion with your work as well.

How to Get the Most out of Your Memberships

Now that you have found some great groups to join to help with your networking, you can just sit back and enjoy, right? Wrong. To be successful at networking, you need to continue to work at it, and you will need to continue to work at your memberships and groups that you have joined. Here are some tips to help you stay in the loop and get the most out of your memberships:

1. **Go** — If you do not go to the meetings and invest your time, you will not become successful at networking with your new groups. Make sure you attend meetings, events, and any other special functions that your organization holds to keep your name and face in front of people.

2. **Do** — By staying involved in the organization, you will start to take on a leadership role in the eyes of others. Start small, by volunteering to lead groups or committees, and move up from there. The more that you do in an organization, the more people will know you and remember you.

3. **Keep Up** — No matter how many people you network with at your new organizations or groups, keep a notebook of information about them for your follow-ups. Follow-ups can be anything from a visit to a phone call to an email. When you follow up, make sure you add in something personal that you remembered when you spoke to them. This will let your contacts know that you really were listening, and that you are a real person, not just a salesperson.

Finding the Center

It is not hard to spot the center of influence in any group. These are the people who are so well connected that everyone knows them and trusts them. Events, groups, and special functions all seem to revolve around them and other people gravitate toward them. These people stand out from all the others, and come across as the most sociable people in the group. If they speak or make a point at a meeting, everyone stops to listen to them.

When you approach these people, they are normally more than happy to help pull you into their existing network. And, the more that you connect with them, the further they pull you in. The further that you get pulled in, the faster you will become a center of influence yourself.

Some of the most powerful centers of influence include writers, speakers, editors, industry pundits, and industry Web entrepreneurs. Keep an eye out for these people who help to speak about, interpret, and shape the market that you seek, as these are the people who start the trends in the industries. Seek them out, and get on their good side. When you can gain their trust, you can begin to be pulled into their huge networking arena and they will also start to spread the word about you as well.

Make the Most of It

When you decide to join a group or purchase a membership, make sure that you are ready to take the time needed to truly make a name for yourself and your business within the group. Show up to the meetings, and make sure that you offer your opinions or help wherever you can. Get yourself involved with their special groups, leadership, and other special events they host or provide for the community. When you make yourself involved with other members, you will find awesome ways of networking that you did not realize were there. Also, make sure you follow up with different contacts that you make in the group. Follow up with them on a friendlier basis — offer to get together for lunch or a golf game, and keep any appointments that you make with members of the group or organization that you join.

By simply following these tips and steps, you will find that you can easily find groups, organizations, and other areas to network in that you never imagined. This will help to boost your business's visibility and credibility, as well as help you make plenty of great business contacts that can help to send you referrals and gain more VIP clients for your growing business.

For business owners, the power to network and make their business visible to everyone that they can takes effort. As a business owner, when you take an active part in your business and how it is marketed, you can begin to work on other ways that you can get your business out and in front of the right people. All business owners need to make contacts that will help them to gain more referrals, cooperation, and to help get your business name out in front of more people. This chapter will help you find ways to make your business visible to all.

The Wonder of the Internet

The Internet is a vast wonderland of games, information, entertainment, business, friends, and family. But, the Internet is so much more to a business owner if you take advantage of it. By pumping up your online networking skills, you will open up a wider world of networking contacts than you could have ever dreamed of.

With the boom of chat rooms, online communities, forums, and more, business owners have access to an almost endless way to network and get their name and business name out there. Online networking, or cybernetworking, helps you to escape the humdrum of the meeting scene and some of the other limitations that come along with meeting people face to face all the time. There are several different areas that you can search for networking groups, but they all will fall into three main categories:

1. **Email Groups** — Also known as listservs, these allow members to join a group of people who all have the same interests. These email groups send out messages that the members post monthly, weekly, or even daily, and each member is encouraged to participate in the discussion. For email groups that relate to a topic you might be interested in, you can visit Topica at **www.topica.com**.

2. **Forums** — Forums, or bulletin boards, have been around for a long time and are specialized Web sites that are usually moderated by an owner or host. These forums allow many group members to post messages at the same time, and are generally a faster way to network than email groups. For a large list of forums, you can go to Delphi Forums at **www.delphiforums.com**.

3. **Newsgroups** — While these are very similar to a forum, they are usually not moderated. You can find thousands of different newsgroups all over the world on about every subject that you can imagine. You will need a newsreader, which comes with most email programs, to read and participate in these newsgroups. One of the best sites to find newsgroups is DejaNews which is found at **www.dejanews.com**.

When you jump into online networking, make sure you follow the same rules that you would if you were meeting someone face to face. A little courtesy goes a long way, and you should not use online networking as a pushy way to shove your business in people's faces. Networking online is about expanding your network in a way that will help you. You do not want to do any damage to your business or reputation by becoming one of those pushy salespeople who send out spam to your contacts.

Referrals, Referrals, Referrals

One of the main reasons that you need to work on networking and keeping a good reputation with people is so they will refer other people to you. When you network with people, you create a trust with them that bleeds over into their business and personal life. This trust is what drives people to refer others to certain businesses or people. The more people you meet and the more people you show that you are trustworthy, the more referrals you will get. You will begin to develop a business relationship with those people as well, so that when they hear a friend, family member, or business associate say that they need a service you provide, your name will come to mind immediately.

The most important thing about a referral is that the person is coming to you already knowing what you do, and is ready to do business.

You will not have to do a lot of educating on what you do or how you do it, and you will not have to do a lot of selling to them to get them to purchase your services — they come to you, primed and ready to go.

Plus, a referral-based business is one that is steady and solid. You have a constant stream of people who come through your door, already knowing what you do and already wanting your services. You do not have to worry about what they know, or do not know, if they heard all about your business through the greatest marketing system on Earth — word of mouth. Any business that can be built up on referral business is one that has unlimited growth potential.

Gaining Referrals

When a client is referred to you, they come to you ready to do business and they already know what you do and how you do it. Chances are they already know whether you are good at what you do or if you lack in some areas. Most of your current clients are more than happy to refer people to you, if you truly deserve it. But why would they do that if they do not get anything in return? Well, most people view a good referral as a way to make them look good or important in another person's eyes. If they can provide a good solution to a problem that a friend has, it makes them a better friend.

Referrals are simply the best way to gain new clients, but it seems that most businesses do not utilize this asset as much as they should. Start to envision your business clients and your business network as a breeding ground for referrals. Referrals come from clients who are happy with your services, no matter if they used you once or every week. Referrals also come from your business network and business associates, since these people know you on a personal level.

There are some simple steps that you can take to pump up your referrals and get this area of your business pulling in more new business.

1. **Build client and contact trust.** Your clients will not refer anyone else to you if they do not trust you. When you are networking, do not be pushy or just hand out business cards. Go out of your way to do something nice, connect with that person on a personal level, or take your time speaking to people so that you gain more quality contacts than quantity. Once you have established a good relationship with your contact, then, and only then, should you consider asking them for referrals. You will not get any referrals from someone you just met, and you will not get quality referrals from passing out business cards to a room full of people.

2. **Ask for referrals.** When you are speaking to your current clients, contacts, vendors, or other people that you know and that trust you, simply ask for their business or referrals. You may be surprised at the results you get from simply asking those people you already know and trust for referrals. But you need to be completely clear on what you are asking before you do it. Be specific as to what you are looking for, or what you need. When people are sure of what you want, they will be better able to find friends, family members, or contacts that they can refer to you.

3. **Create a referral reward program.** You will be amazed at what a small plaque in your office lobby can do for your referral business. When people see that they will be acknowledged for referring people to you, or that they will gain discounts, prizes, or free services, they will begin

to refer more people to you as well. Look at your business and see what type of referral program may fit the best, and then implement it. Let your current clients and customers know you are starting up this program, and offer them special incentives to refer people to you.

4. **Remember to acknowledge the client.** This is probably the biggest mistake that people make when it comes to referrals. Your clients want to know you appreciate them referring their friends, family, business associates, and others to you. So you need to make sure you show them you appreciate their generosity. Simple thank-you notes, phone calls, or other small ways of showing that you appreciate their help is a great way to let them know. But if you find that a client or other contact has just referred a large group or big area of business to you, then you should take the appropriate steps to ensure that you return their kindness. You should tailor your thank you to the size and scope of the referral.

When you are able to put all of the steps in this chapter to work for you successfully, then you will begin to see your business grow by leaps and bounds. Make sure you follow up as completely as you can, and enlist help or hire new employees if you find you are overwhelmed on this front. Do not let opportunities pass you by, and do not forget to thank those who send the opportunities your way. In the next chapter, you will learn to make your business stand out from all the others, and help you get ahead of the pack when it comes to visibility.

Chapter 12: Forming Alliances With Vendors

"Strategic partnerships" is what this chapter is all about, and how to find them where you probably would not expect them — with your vendors. All across the business world, smart business owners are forming alliances with other companies to help forge mutually beneficial alliances. This practice is becoming the norm and publications are starting to pick up on it. According to *The Economist*, business alliances now make up 18 percent of the revenue of America's largest companies. These "strategic partnerships" include co-op advertising with partners, sponsorships, cause-related marketing, and cross-promoting products or services. While each business continues to represent themselves, they also represent their partners with just as much zeal.

It does not matter if you are partnering with a manufacturer of the components that make up your bestselling item, members of your local Chamber of Commerce, or a company that sells you cleaning supplies — forming alliances with vendors can have a great effect on your business and theirs.

Linking up with these businesses can help you create roads to new markets by combining your skills and marketing efforts, as well as your smarts, talents, and capabilities to reach different target markets.

And they may be interested in an alliance for potential value that you can add for them in one or more areas.

If you are not sure about forming alliances with vendors, take a look at your own business challenges. Are there business expenses that you can share with the company you partner with? Or are there goods or services that you can provide each other to create better businesses on both ends? Sometimes it is simply that you want to ride their coattails as they earn business, and at other times you want to lead the pack and allow others to piggy-back on your success. Either way you look at it, forming alliances with vendors will help to create more visibility and a better reliability on your business in your target market.

So how do you go about finding potential partners? Begin with talking to your suppliers and looking for worthwhile businesses that already serve the same target market you do. Network at trade associations and meetings, and feel around for the best possible vendors to partner with. When you find them, look for ways to pool your talents, abilities, and other assets together to create a win-win for you both. There are several different ways that you can forms these alliances with vendors, such as co-branding, cause-related, and even cross-promotions.

Forming a Co-Branding Alliance

Co-branding is about piggy-backing on each other's marketing, or marketing two complementary products together. This is a great way to form an alliance with a vendor, since most vendor products and your business services will go hand-in-hand. Thus, if one has a good reputation and the other is just starting out, that new business can ride on the success of the first one. Or you can pool your marketing together and gain better prospects from several target markets at the same time. For this type of alliance to be successful, both businesses will need to share the costs of marketing and will need to see more success than they would have alone.

Forming a Cause-Related Alliance

A cause-related alliance is a business and a special cause or charity joining together to market their image, product, or service so that both can benefit. This can be a great way for both to succeed, as most consumers would much rather do business with a company that stands for more than just profit. When you identify a cause that you are pairing with, make sure you identify the media so you can reap the benefits of the pairing. One of the best ways of establishing a cause-related alliance is to establish a relationship with a charitable organization.

Forming Cross-Promotions

These are strategies that are formed to align businesses that serve the same target market, but do not compete with each other — such as a vendor, who provides the main component for your product, and your business sharing an advertising campaign. Cross-promotional marketing helps you reach a much larger audience with less effort and less money, because two companies pool their resources, such as time, ideas, contacts, and money.

Cross-promotional marketing can help everyone involved to:

- Conserve resources, such as cash.

- Generate more reasons for your target market to purchase your services.

- Stand out in an overcrowded marketplace and give your business extra visibility in other markets as well.

- Show your support for community causes that your target market cares about.

- Build your business's credibility with your target market.

- Reach out to more prospects.

Be creative in your cross-promotional marketing strategies. For example, it is a simple way to build holiday sales by joining forces with local businesses, such as restaurants, book shops, card shops, and florists for Valentine's Day if you offer services like marriage counseling.

There are thousands of ways that you can form alliances with your vendors. Be creative in forming alliances and in marketing endeavors, as there are also hundreds of other businesses out there that will be forming alliances as well. By staying creative in your alliances and the ways that you market your business, you will reach all of the markets you are targeting.

Chapter 13: Learn the Art of the Article

Most business owners still have not mastered one of the greatest marketing tools in the world — the article. You do not have to be a professional writer to create a great article that will get your name in print. But you should have a knowledge base about the subject you are going to write about before you crank a few out. It does not matter if you are a consultant or a salesperson; publishing articles under your name will do wonders for your business. And with all the different publications that are on the market today, it is becoming easier to get an article published.

Publishers Need Your Articles

Almost every publication out there today, from newsletters to magazines, has a wide variety of writers that they depend on for information, and the vast majority of them are freelance writers. These writers provide everything from the feature article in a large magazine to simple filler work in smaller ones. In today's business world, you no longer have to have an agent or have a family member in a publishing company to gain access to this awesome marketplace. You simply need to learn the rules of the freelance market and follow them.

This chapter presents a step-by-step process of how to get your articles in publications that will reach the target market you seek. Once you have this down, you will find that you can place articles in all types of publications on a consistent basis, which will help you to bring in new business contacts and make vital connections in the business world.

Becoming a Published Expert

Bylined articles are becoming one of the staples of business publications. Usually, these articles are written for a small fee, or sometimes simply given in exchange for an author bio or byline at the bottom of the article to help drive in business. No matter what is done in exchange for these articles, they are designed to show off your business expertise.

Step One: Keep It Small — When you begin your trek on writing articles for publications as an expert, keep your expectations realistic. Usually, new authors assume their articles will publish in a top-of-the-line publication that everyone has heard of, and that they will receive some outrageous pay for it. This could not be further from the truth. This is like a rookie football player expecting to start every quarter of every game and getting a veteran's salary. It does not happen. Most of the huge publications are completely staff written, and it is extremely hard for any freelance writer to break into them.

On the other hand, there are many smaller publications that you can easily submit articles to and get them to notice. Smaller trade-oriented publications are always looking for contributing authors, even if the pay is small or nonexistent. These publications normally cater to a small target market that you can use to help push your business and promote yourself as an expert. The editors at these publications are normally a lot more accessible to a writer than those of a larger publication, and you will probably have a much easier time getting something in print in one of them.

Step Two: Creating Great Article Ideas — Your next step will be to come up with some interesting article topics that your target market will find helpful. You do not have to strain your imagination, nor do you have to research for months before you can write something good. Simply study the publications that you are considering sending articles to so you can get a feel for what they will, and will not, publish. Keep an eye out for new patterns or trends in your field, and create articles that will play up the new ones that you are interested in.

Keep any relevant articles or other publications that fit into your "expert" area as launching points or ready-made research. Then, when you are ready to create an article, you will have all your information ready to go and it will not take you long to research and write.

Step Three: The Difference in a Story Idea and Just a Topic — "Marketing" or "sales" is too broad a topic for you to pitch to an editor. Instead, you need to bring that broad topic down into a workable idea that you can easily pitch to any editor. Even though you can still connect your article to the larger topic that you are interested in, break it down and focus on one particular area of that article. Look at the topic you want to write about from many different angles until you can find one that will allow you to place it in a smaller section for a publication. For example, if you are writing a smaller, 500-word article, you need to find one aspect of your topic and focus in extremely close on that aspect.

For a larger, 2,000-word article, you can have a broader view, but you will still need to bring the topic down to that level.

Step Four: Studying a Publication — As you are doing your homework to start pitching ideas to editors, you need to make sure you have a copy of their publication so you can study the types of articles they print. You can easily pick one up from your local bookstore, or call the publisher to request a sample, or order one from them directly online. It is also a great idea to contact the publisher and ask for their writer's guidelines, their editorial schedule (such as when they like to have new articles submitted by), and a small index of recently published articles. This is not the time for you to pitch ideas to them, simply ask for these things and say thank you.

Once you have your samples, take the time to look through each one of the publications that you have your eye on. Study the style of the publication, their focus on a specific industry or area, and their take on different ideas. Then you will be able to slant your work to fit what they are printing and their style so that you have a much better chance of being published with them.

Step Five: Selling Your Work — Most professional writers will try to sell an idea before they actually sit down and write. They normally do not develop an article, write it, and then send it in to several publishers before they sell it. Why? Because most editors want to be able to have to input on the article that can help shape it to their publication. There are certain steps you will need to go through to gain an editor's trust and have the communication lines open up before you start writing away. So before you start cranking out articles and sending them off randomly, you need to start with a simple way of communicating with the publication and the editors.

Step Six: The Query Letter — A query letter is the best way to start the dialog with you and an editor. This letter sums up what you want to write about and why you are qualified to do so, like a miniproposal. It helps to sell you, your work, your business, and your expertise on the subject so that the editor will want to publish your work. In a way, this is like a cold call, but it is the best way to get your foot in the door with a publisher. There are plenty of great Web sites that can help you create the perfect query letter for your idea, and it is best to visit a few of them and learn exactly what you need to do. Practice writing query letters and have a friend or family member read them and give you pointers on where you can change information or place in more information.

Make sure, when you are sending out your query letter, that you take the time to find out who the managing editor is and use their name on the query letter itself. You should never send a generic query letter that just says "Dear Editor" or "Dear Publisher." These show that you have not placed a lot of time into your letter and they will assume you have not done much with your idea or writing as well.

Keep your letter, and your letterhead, professional. You do not need to send a query letter on flowery stationery or some other type of paper that is less than you would place a resume on. Also, you want to keep your presentation as crisp and clear as possible. You do not need to go on about items that will not make a difference in your article or in your pitch to the editor. If you have special credentials that will lend to your expertise in writing the article, you should highlight them, but do not rattle on about personal problems or items that do not relate to your article.

Step Seven: After the Letter Is Sent — Once you have taken the time to craft your article idea and draft a great query letter, it is time to send it out. After it is sent, then what do you do? There are three different things that will happen at this point:

1. **Your query will be rejected.** Do not take this personally. Sometimes they already have their calendars full, or your style did not fit with their publication. It does not mean your writing was horrible. Just send it on to the next publication.

2. **You will not hear anything at all.** If you do not hear from a publication or editor in about three to four weeks, send a follow-up message to them as a reminder. If another three or four weeks go by, then you can call the editor.

3. **You will get a thumbs-up from the editor on "speculation,"** which means the editor likes your idea and wants you to go ahead and write the article. But, they will not commit to publishing it until they have the article to read and edit. This means you need to do the best possible writing you can, so your article will get published.

Step Eight: Writing — Now that you have sold your article idea to a publisher, it is time to gather your research and your wits and head to the computer. Make sure you have a clear layout of the editor's schedule, time line, or other date that he or she needs the work completed by for publication. The editor should have given you an idea of how long he or she would like the article to be, and you should stick to this like glue.

The first thing is to create an outline of how the article will flow and develop. This is like a blueprint for your article and you should not start writing until you have this ready. A good outline will also help stop writer's block and help you to organize your research so you can create an awesome article that will be accepted with no question.

Once you have your outline ready, get your research in order so that you can fly through your writing with little distraction by searching for the item you wanted to use or quote. By having everything on hand, you can easily write without problem.

Step Nine: Rights and Contracts — This is the part that you need to know in and out. Once you have your work accepted and bought by a publisher, it is no longer free domain for you to post anywhere unless stated as such in your contract with the publisher. There are several different types of copyrights and contracts that editors use, and here are a few of the most common ones and what they entail:

1. **First rights** — This means that when the publication buys the rights, they get the right to publish it before anyone else and they have the exclusive right to use the article for the life of the issue where it will appear. Once this issue is not current, you can them republish it.

2. **One-time rights** — This means that the publisher will publish it once. The writer can sell the work to multiple publications at one time, but you need to have a clear schedule of when and where the work will be published.

3. **All rights** — This means you are completely signing over the article to the publisher in a specific period that is defined by copyright law. With this arrangement, the publisher will own all rights to the work, and you will have to gain permission to use it, or any part of it, elsewhere.

4. **Work for hire** — This means you will sell your copyright and the claim on this article forever. This is usually the way that ghost writing is done. They will then completely own the copyright and they do not have to put your name

on the work. This is not the way you want to go if you are trying to get your name in print.

5. **Electronic rights** — This means that the publisher is purchasing the right to place the work online or in another electronic form. When you agree to this, make sure you also have the ability to reuse your work in any form.

You should be clear on what your rights to the work will be once it has been accepted and published, and you should not hesitate to ask questions if you do not understand something. The editor will send you a contract, which you will sign and return to them before any work is printed or paid for. Once you have everything signed and sent, it is time to sit back and watch your work go up in print.

In the next chapter, we will examine how to use other forms of media to your advantage so you can gain from the publicity that they can provide without a lot of effort.

Chapter 14: Learn to Use the Media to Your Advantage

Think about all the media that is out there — television, radio, print, and the Internet. These make for a ton of media opportunities that you should take advantage of to help promote yourself and your business. This chapter will show you how to use the media to your advantage so you can gain free advertising and get your name and your business name out there for more people to see. But as with any other part of this book, it works the best when you are familiar with the channels that you want to use and how they work.

Build a Media File

One of the first major steps in using the media to your advantage is to create a file that has up-to-date information about the different media outlets that you want to target. Know the key people in those organizations that reach your target market the most and how to contact them to let them know about any media-worthy event you are holding. Your main goal is to build a list of areas that you would like to have media coverage in.

You can start your research by asking some of your clients what their favorite publications are, what they watch the most, what radio station they listen to, and where they get news that relates to your industry. Follow up this information with either a trip to the library or a couple of hours researching those publications online, so that you can familiarize yourself with the media resources that are available in those different media organizations.

While you are doing your media file research, you will be amazed at the large number of publications that are extremely specific on certain aspects of your business and industry. This can also be a great way to find publishers to market your articles to. Get to know the different ways that you can search for new media outlets, both online and offline. This way, you can find new and updated information on a constant basis without wasting a lot of time looking.

It does not matter if you only serve a specialized target market; you should be able to find several different media outlets that you can use to your advantage. So do not limit yourself to local media only. You should always be looking for opportunities to broaden your exposure with different media outlets that have a national reach. Even if this exposure will not lead to direct sales, it can help to establish you as an expert and gain credibility with your target market.

Study Your Target Media Markets

Now that you have the names and contact information for potential media outlets, you should get to know some of the most promising ones first-hand. If they are available locally, you should purchase a few of the publications, watch the programs, or listen to that radio station. Once you are sure this is a media outlet that you can use to your advantage to reach your target market, you can research to get the names of the key people at each one. These will be the editors and people on the news side of the media, like reporters, editors, producers, and writers. You do not need to contact the sales reps or the publishers who deal with the business areas of the media.

Keep yourself familiarized with each media outlet that you feel can help you reach that target market. Listen, watch, or read them on a constant basis and be able to jump on opportunities that can offer you great coverage on any type of event. Once you have studied these media outlets, you will have a good idea of whom to approach and how to do it to gain media coverage.

Press Kits and Other Media Materials

Before you start to approach any type of media outlet for a story, you should have several introductory packages about your business ready to go. These are called press kits. Depending on your business and the image that you want to convey, these kits can range from elaborate to simple. No matter your style, there are some things you should always have included in your kits:

1. Your company background information

2. News releases with current information about your business

3. Biographies of your company's principals

4. A one-page "fact sheet" about your business

5. A FAQ sheet — like a mock interview

6. A photo(s) of your business or you

7. Copies of articles you have written

8. Customer references and testimonials

9. A list of any past media coverage with samples

A good rule of thumb is to keep your kits simple, which means you should include just enough information to introduce the media to you and to your business. Make sure you include any necessary background information about your company and you that is relevant to media coverage, and ensure that you make a good impression. Remember that you will not be sending out these kits all the time; these will only be on a request basis from a reporter or other media professional.

With the Internet becoming one of the most universal media coverage venues, you should learn how to create these media kits online as well. An online media kit will contain the same information as a traditional one, just in a browsable form, such as on an area of your Web site, which is called an online press room.

Since journalists have the freedom to help themselves to anything in an online press room, you should include everything that you can about your business. This means you should have everything on the list above and more, such as white papers, company positioning statements, and press statements. A great way to place all of this information online is to put it into a PDF file that can be easily downloaded and printed by media personnel.

Introduce Yourself and Your Business as an Expert Source

All writer, reporters, and producers need to form relationships with outside experts that they can call on when they need an expert opinion. You can easily become one of these experts simply by letting the right people know about you and your business, and making a great case to them that you are the expert that they should consult when they need you.

The best way to begin this process is to identify the media professionals who are most likely to need your expert opinion. For instance, journalists who cover medical topics would want to find experts in all different areas of medicine, and if you are a surgeon, they can use you as an expert for any story they are covering that deals with your area. But it is not just as simple as calling them up and telling them you are an expert. You need to make contact with them and introduce yourself to them. Give them the qualifications that make you an expert in your field and offer your help to them if they ever need it for a story. You can also let them know that you would like an alert occasionally when they are covering stories that relate to your area.

Make sure you approach media contacts as you would a new client. You should convey to them that you are here to solve their problems and that their audience needs the specific information only you can provide.

Above everything else, the media contacts you make need to know you are credible. This means if someone you speak to in the media is receptive to you and your information, send them out a press kit to show you are the type of business owner or professional they can depend on when they need information.

Once you have your media contacts receptive to your information and help, you can then send out press releases and other useful information when you are holding an event or when new information comes out about your industry. By keeping a great relationship going with your media contacts, you will find that you can gain great free coverage from them when you need it most.

Chapter 15

Some Pitfalls to Avoid

Like every other thing you do in life, there will always be a trial-and-error period that you have to go through before you hammer out all the kinks. But to help you avoid some of the bigger ones to keeping you motivated and on the right track, here are some of the major pitfalls to avoid while you build up yourself, your brand, and your business.

A Few Things to Keep in Mind

1. **People will imitate you**. If you become successful in your personal branding, someone, somewhere, will try to copy something you have done. While they may not have my book to guide them along, they will not have the same advantage that you do. And you will have another advantage that they will not — you were the first and the original. The good thing about being the first one to do what you have done is that it will only make anyone else who tries to copy you actually look like they are copying you, and will only succeed in making them be more of a follower than a leader in the field. You should always make sure the people who are

in your target market know that the newcomer is only an imitation, and you are the original.

2. **All competitors have a weakness.** No matter if you are trying to earn the top spot in your field, or if you find an imitator who is digging in his or her heels, keep in mind that all businesses have a weakness. You need to study this competitor and you will find it. It can be as simple as arrogance or poor creative work or it can be as big as a past scandal — study the business and the owner, and you will find it. Remember that you are not in business to be friends with everyone else; you are in business to be the best.

3. **Some people will look at you with scorn** — especially if you become successful. Remember that there will always be someone — clients, other professionals, and even prospects — that will look at your personal brand or your marketing with scorn. Normally this is just a little envy coming out from another competitor who did not think of your idea first or who does not have the guts to do what you are doing. Do not get discouraged by this. There is a reason you are successful and they are not, so keep on doing what you are doing, and let them keep doing what they are doing — it will make it easier to grab their clients.

4. **Spend the extra money on good quality printing.** No matter where else in your budget you can save money, you should always spend the extra money on good quality printing. The overall look and feel of your materials will say just as much about you and your business as any of the designs and written items will. Do not skimp on the

printing costs, no matter how tempting the offer. When some printer tries to sell you cheap paper, make sure that you do not take the bait. When you get that box of beautiful brochures, businesses cards, or other marketing materials and they do not feel like colored tissue paper, then you will know you made the right choice.

5. **Constantly think about how you can add more value to your services.** By continually changing how you can add more value to your services, you will gain new customers by showing them that they get a little bit extra from you than the competition. Think about special things that you can provide them that will help them see that you are the best, such as: special reports, free subscriptions to special publications, free software, free seminar invitations, or even free gift certificates. Ask yourself the following questions constantly: What can I promise to a client who will give me a great referral, and what extra benefits can I offer to prospective clients to get them to call me for an appointment? By constantly staying on top of what extra things you can provide, you will always be the best choice for both existing and new clients.

6. **Underpromise and then overdeliver to clients.** For example, do not tell clients and prospects that you are the greatest thing since sliced bread. Tell them instead that you are "good" at what you do. Then deliver services to them like you are the greatest thing they have ever come across. By underpromising and overdelivering, you will ensure that your clients see the value of your services and you will still be able to manage their expectations of you and your business. This is one of the most powerful ways that you can build a great database of clients who

simply fall in love with you and will remain loyal to you forever.

7. **Make sure that you keep the most up-to-date materials for clients to keep them interested.** Make sure you make changes to your brochures, postcards, direct mailers, and other marketing materials at least once or twice a year. When you can keep things fresh and new, it will continue to catch the attention of those who are already your clients and will always catch new clients who did not notice you before.

8. **Do not go after too many new prospects.** Remember how we learned about narrowing down your target market? This is so you do not overload yourself and then destroy your business by not being able to deliver what you promised. If you develop your brand and your business correctly and you are targeting the right market, it will flood you with business and you will not have to worry about marketing to too many places.

9. **Never stop being a salesperson.** Keep in mind that just your personal brand will not close the sale for anyone. The purpose of your brand is to get the right people in your door, and to get about 90 percent of those people ready to sign up with you. But you still have to close the deal for them. Remember that selling is your job, so always work on your selling pitch and your sales skills. Make sure you are ready to treat people like golden nuggets when they walk through your door so they will never leave you.

10. **Your business staff is the most important people you have.** What? Not clients? That is right! The employees of your business are the most important people in your

business. If you take great care of your staff, treat them right, and make sure they have what they need to do their jobs right, they will treat your clients right and handle them with care. This is why you should always hire people with care and then reward them for helping to build your business and make your brand more successful. Bonuses are a great way to help employees stay motivated, and you can always offer special things to employees who go above and beyond the call of duty. Make your employees work as a team, encourage them to help come up with new ways and ideas, and genuinely listen to them. Form a great staff that loves you, and they will make your job 100 percent easier.

A Few Things to Avoid

Of course, there are a few things you should always avoid with all your might. Here are some of the most common mistakes that new business owners make that can cause them some major headaches, if not undo all the hard work that they have already done:

1. **Do NOT show any of your branding materials, logos, or other items to your competition or colleagues BEFORE you print it.** Not only do you run the risk of someone stealing your ideas, you will only get a bunch of lame advice that you did not want and a ton of negative ideas about it. Just get them where you are perfectly happy with them and print. Then show them to your colleagues. By showing them before they are printed, you will start to second-guess yourself and your brand. So just do not do it.

2. **Do not copy after someone else.** This is one of the things that can break your business before you even get off the

ground. You will be surprised at how tempting it is to copy someone's brand or logo. But when you have been working hard on your brand for months and just barely getting business, then some new business comes along and starts stealing all the business, it is tempting to copy what they are doing. Just resist the temptation and do not do it. You will not gain anything by copying someone else except a reputation for being unoriginal.

3. **Do not give out "tacky" items with your promotional stuff.** Things like mugs, memo pads, magnets, and such do not do a lot to help your brand identity. They only make your business look cheap and you do not want that. Let the other guys do this and boost your reputation by giving items that are more in line for higher quality clients, like tie pins, high-quality ink pens, and even money clips.

4. **Do not think like a simple sole proprietor, think like a business.** If you are going to put in the time and the hard work to create a personal brand, then run yourself like a business. It will make you a lot more efficient and when your marketing gains momentum, it will help things go more smoothly. Also, if your brand takes off, you will be dealing with more and more clients, so running like a business will also help streamline that process as well. Think big and be big.

5. **Do NOT ignore the Internet or what it can do for you.** In today's business world, you have to have a professional email account and you have to have a Web site. Just bite the bullet and do it. Aside from that, do not forget what a great resource the Internet is when it comes to providing information for prospects and clients 24 hours a day.

6. **Do not be afraid to try new things.** Just because you do not see it in this book, or you have not heard of anyone else doing it, does not mean that it will not work for you. If a wild idea hits you and you think you can pull it off, go for it! Do not be afraid to break out of the box and do something different.

7. **Last — do not panic if your business does not take off the first day you are open.** It takes time to get your brand out there, and you should not panic and change your whole strategy if business is not beating down your door right away. No matter how good your brand is and how great your marketing is, it will take a bit for people to notice you, so do not worry too much. Put at least six months into your branding efforts before you change directions.

These are some of the major pitfalls to avoid, and information that all business owners should remember and follow. Just keeping these few things in mind will help save you from some of the major problems that other businesses face all the time and keep your business on the top of the pack.

In the next part of the book, we will learn how you can start to pull in clients with the hard work that you have put in so far. Marketing is a huge thing in business, and you have to know how to market your business, what areas to market the most, and where you should market to gain those VIP clients that you desire. Part Three of this book will take you through the marketing basics that you need to live by to gain more exposure and clients.

Part Three

Grabbing Your First Clients

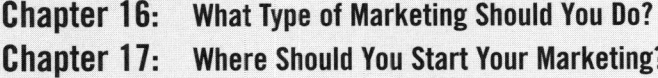

Chapter 16: What Type of Marketing Should You Do?
Chapter 17: Where Should You Start Your Marketing?
Chapter 18: Marketing Success Ingredients
Chapter 19: Creating a Winning Plan
Chapter 20: Setting Goals and Keeping Them
Chapter 21: Making Contacts and Appointments
Chapter 22: Keeping Track of Your Contacts
Chapter 23: Following Up With Contacts After the Appointment

When it comes to grabbing your first clients, you have to remember that they will not just come beating your door down because you just opened up. You must have completed the previous steps in the book and have a good, credible, and professional business appearance to help clients and prospects know you are here to stay and not be gone tomorrow. Clients will want to know that you can provide the services that they need, and that you will not be gone next week or next year.

Another large part of building your business is marketing. This is the main way that you grab clients and reel them in. This part of the book will go through the basics of marketing and show you how to market your business, where to market it, and what you should and should not do. Many business owners assume they know how to market their business when they actually have no clue what they are doing. By knowing what to do and how to do it, you will automatically have a jump on your competition that will help you succeed in bringing in those VIP clients from your target market.

But marketing is not the only thing that you need to concentrate on when it comes to winning your first clients. There are many other areas that go into getting clients and taking care of them. We will also go through what you should do after you start bringing in clients and making appointments. To be a professional business, you need to run like one and appear like one. We will help you find what it is that you need to do to ensure you treat your first clients right.

So now we head into the next chapter in the book, "What Type of Marketing Should You Do?" which will go through the basics of marketing, what it is, and which type you should engage in.

Chapter 16: What Type of Marketing Should You Do?

Let us start with the real question here: Just what is marketing? Marketing is telling people — potential clients — what you do, over and over and over again. There are numerous ways of marketing, or telling people what you do, and it does not matter what kind of marketing you choose, but you do have to do it. You cannot just open up your business and then sit by the phone and wait for business to flow in; it does not happen. You have to market your business and yourself. Some marketing firms say the average American will see over 4,000 marketing messages each day. Where will yours fit into that list? Will they remember it, or toss it out with the rest of the garbage that they hear during the day?

Getting clients to open up and listen to what you are telling them, and remember what you say, is the challenge. It can seem like an overwhelming one, but it does not have to be. Start by taking a look at how other professionals in your field gain their clients. Ask any successful professional that question and you will probably hear a wide variety of responses: "Making contacts and following up with them," "Networking," or even "Referrals." There is probably no end to the different ways that people will pull clients in and you can use all, or only some, of them.

Marketing is actually pretty simple stuff, and you probably already knew what those answers would be before you even read that sentence, right? So why is it that you do not have the VIP clients that you want and need in your office, booking your appointment calendar solid? See if any of these reasons sound familiar to you:

1. **You do not know where to start.** Marketing can seem like an overwhelming project and there are almost too many ideas to consider when you are starting out. You want to make sure you are making the right choices so you constantly worry about how to start out and where to spend your marketing dollars first. So you simply flip back and forth on marketing ideas, and end up doing nothing.

2. **You cannot keep yourself motivated with marketing.** Even if you knew where to start and what to do, you cannot get it all done. You no longer have a boss over your shoulder, waiting on a report from you on your progress, and it is so easy to avoid marketing and sales since most people do not like to do it. Or, you started out strong, but did not see immediate results and now you have slacked off.

3. **You just are not quite sure how to put all the marketing pieces together.** Should you start with cold calls? Your Web site? Gain new leads? Network? Sometimes finding the right place to dig in and make it all work can overwhelm anyone and you are not sure which puzzle pieces go together well and which do not.

If any of these fit you, do not worry. You are not alone in this. Most people who market their professional services rarely fail due to the lack of basic information about marketing. They fail because they do not use the information they have right there in front of them. But with the help of this book, you will learn how to get your marketing tool kit ready to go, and how to use it successfully so you will become a marketing guru in your field.

The next time you worry about what type of marketing you should do, you will already know the answer to that question and be able to jump right into the marketing world and get it done. Our next chapter will show you where you should start your marketing, the first main tool in your marketing tool box.

Chapter 17
Where Should You Start Your Marketing?

This chapter will help you answer the question of where to start your marketing efforts. For every type of business, there will be so many different starting points that it can get overwhelming. And for every business owner, there will be certain areas of marketing that he or she does not feel comfortable with. So business owners will start in a different place when they begin beginning marketing their business to their target market.

The solution to taking the jumble of different starting points to your marketing — and creating a good starting point for you and your business — is to break down each different marketing avenue that is open to you and lay out a "menu" for your marketing.

Think of your marketing plan as more like a gourmet meal for your business. You want to carefully plan out each course and what goes into it, just as you would if you were cooking for a special person. Once you lay out your menu, it is time to shop for the highest-quality ingredients to go into your menu items, and then you need to figure out how to combine everything to make the menu flow together seamlessly. To come up with this "menu" for your marketing, I am going to help you create a marketing strategy that you can follow to get your marketing juices flowing in the right direction.

What Is a Marketing Strategy?

A marketing strategy is the base for your whole marketing plan — your marketing budget, marketing avenues, how you start your marketing, who you market to, and so on. You can always look back at your marketing strategy when you get sidetracked or if you are trying to decide which marketing tactic to employ next.

Every marketing strategy is made up of more than one tactic. These chosen tactics make up the basis for your marketing network, and give you something to work with when one tactic does not seem to be pulling in the business you had hoped. This is essentially your marketing toolbox and the marketing tools to build your client base.

I will go through some of the main marketing strategies that most business owners use to pull in clients in the next chapter, "Marketing Success Ingredients." I will describe them a bit, so you know what goes into each one and what you will need to do to implement it in your marketing arsenal. Do not worry about picking out specific marketing strategies right now; instead, take a good look at each of the strategies mentioned in the next chapter and begin to think about which ones may be right for you.

And now, on to the marketing tools that you will need to build your client base!

Chapter 18

Marketing Success Ingredients

In this chapter, you will learn all about the different marketing tactics and strategies that the majority of successful business owners use in their arsenal. These are proven tactics that have been used over and over. But they do not automatically work when you throw them out there. The key is to use them in the right way for your business.

We will examine each one, and learn the basics about what it is, what it does, and how it can work for your business so you can make an informed decision on which ones will fit into your arsenal and which you may put on the back burner for now. Remember, you do not have to pick out your tools now. Instead, focus on the descriptions and the tactics themselves so you will fully understand them.

Strategy #1: Direct Contacts and Following Up

Everyone knows direct contact means making a personal contact with someone who is a prospective client, either by mail, by phone, by email, by fax, or in person. To get true results from this strategy, you have to make the contact personal, not just a form letter that you found online or a mass email that you had written. Find a way to address the specific person you are trying to reach, such as the CEO of a company, and personalize the contact for them by discussing a problem they are facing. If you cannot find a way to personalize each contact, then you are simply sending out direct mail and most of your efforts will hit the trash bin.

Once you make an initial contact with a person, you can then move to more impersonal items, such as mass mailings or e-zines. But for contacts that are truly interested in your services, you need to be sure that you use these types of follow-up items as a supplement to your personal contact. If you use these as your first contacts, you will not gain any business from them.

Here are some of the tactics you can use for direct contact and follow up:

1. **Cold calling** — Now this one is for true salespeople only. Most people will cringe at the thought of cold calling, but if you can find out information about a complete stranger and tell them why they need your services without any help from them directly, this tactic can work. Of course, there are you sales-types out there who can sell ice cubes to a polar bear, and this can be your bread and butter if worked right.

2. **Warm calling** — This one is a bit easier. You call people that you have already made some type of contact with: either a referral, someone you have already talked to in person, or even someone who belongs to one of the professional or personal community groups that you are a member of. This type of contact is a bit easier, since you already have a base to talk with them about your services.

3. **Appointments** — This can be done in person or over the phone. This is a good way to present your services and what you do in detail, and normally will lead to a formal proposal (for larger business clients) or a sale of your services.

4. **Invitations** — This is a good way to get a lot of prospects into your office or event without doing much work. You send out invitations to a meeting, seminar, or just to your office where you are not hosting any type of sales presentation. This is a great way to meet and gain prospects without being overly pushy on selling to them.

5. **Personal letters or emails** — Sending out personalized letters or emails to a hot prospect can be a great way to reel them in. This is a great way to gain more clients, but the key is that the communications have to really be personalized, and not just a mass email or letter. Then follow up with a phone call to the person in a day or two, to ensure he or she got the email or letter.

6. **Announcement card** — This is a great way to let new prospects know you are opening your doors for the first time. You can offer a special or discount on services that you know people will need, and then follow up with phone calls.

7. **Personal notes** — Sometimes these are termed "nice-to-meet-you-notes" and are sent out after you meet a prospective client and get their information. It is a great way to personalize yourself in their minds and you can also include marketing information for them as well.

8. **Reminder postcards** — This is a great way to let people know that you are still around when you client list becomes larger.

9. **E-zines or newsletters** — A great follow-up tool that you can use to help provide good information to clients and potential clients about things that are relevant to your services. It also helps to show off your expertise in the area and remind people about you and your services.

10. **Lunch appointments** — This is great for larger clients that you are trying to "woo" to your business. You can take them to lunch or coffee as a follow-up tactic. This is a great time to get to know them better and to better explain what you do and what you can offer them.

Strategy #2: Networking and Building Your Referral Base

Recall that we learned about networking and building on your referral base in Chapter 11; we will not go through it over again. But it is very important to remember that networking is one of the marketing strategies you can add to your arsenal and one that I personally recommend highly. It always works as long as you continue to do it and it will not only help your business, but yourself, grow. And by building your network, you continually build your referral base.

Here is a short list to recap the networking tactics to put in your marketing strategy:

1. Attend meetings and seminars to help meet people in your business and those in your target market.

2. Develop referral partners with other vendors who offer services that go hand-in-hand with what you do.

3. Participate in online communities that help to offer networking opportunities and give you more contacts for your business.

4. Take your contacts to lunch or coffee to get to know them better and close larger sales.

5. Stay in touch with former clients to let them know that you still care and that your services are still available to them if they need you.

6. Volunteer and serve on committees in your area to help build your networking and referral base.

7. Share information and resources with other business professionals in your community and ask the same from them.

8. Collaborate with some of your business associates and other professionals in your area to help both of you expand your contacts and networks.

9. Swap contacts with other business professionals who offer services that go hand-in-hand with yours.

10. Give referrals to other business professionals who offer services that go hand-in-hand with yours.

11. Join lead groups to find other professionals who want to exchange leads and contacts.

Strategy #3: Public Speaking Engagements

Some people fear public speaking to the point that they will not even hold a toast at a family event. But public speaking can be a great way to network to a large group of people at one time. People are more likely to remember you and your business if you are standing up in front of them, educating them about something and not sitting in the back of the room, writing notes. If you are new to public speaking or you have a big fear of it, then start out small. Volunteer to help introduce people at an event, offer your services on a panel of specialists, or even hold a small meeting or seminar for some select business contacts. Then you can work your way up to the larger venues and get your word out more.

One word of caution about public speaking though: Seek out already-organized groups to present your seminars or message to instead of inviting random people. You will be surprised at the number of groups and events that eagerly seek out free speakers for their meetings.

Here are some helpful tactics for public speaking:

1. **Host meetings** — Any time you can find a reason to get up in front of a group and speak, it will make you more visible to everyone. Look for opportunities to host meetings or serve on program committees or arrange to help with announcements or other speaking opportunities with groups that you are involved in.

2. **Serve on panels** — This is an easy way to get in front of people without the fear of public speaking. It can help you break into speaking in front of people, and still get your

name out there. It lets people know who you are and that you are available as an expert in your field.

3. **Make presentations** — Just like meetings or conferences, presentations are another great way to get in front of people and break into public speaking. Presentations are geared more to groups, and you can always find groups who are looking for free speakers to host presentations for them.

4. **Virtual speaking** — This is one of the best ways that you wallflowers can break into public speaking without worrying about actually being in front of people. You can hold webinars, tele-seminars, and online chat sessions that are sponsored by associations on your subject to help get your name and business out there.

5. **Give workshops or classes** — If you enjoy speaking in public and you enjoy educating people on items that fit into your range of services or expertise, give workshops or classes. You can offer your services for free to local groups, schools, and organizations. When people see and hear you, they will learn more about you and your services. If they like what they see and hear, they will want more of it.

Strategy #4: Writing and Publicity

Writing different pieces within your area of expertise is a great way to gain publicity and credibility that you could not manage otherwise. There are many different ways that you can create written pieces to publish both online and off — articles, blogs, eBooks, books, newsletters, e-zines, and columns. Many newer Web sites are always in need of new writers who are experts in the areas that they handle, and established Web sites will pay for articles or other written work. Both will help get your name out there and help establish you as an expert in your field. No matter which arena you choose to place your expert skills in written form, make sure you keep a constant stream of work (say one full-length article every two months or so) flowing so people will have your name around constantly.

Do not worry if you are not a good writer. You can always hire an editor or a ghost writer to help sharpen your work and make it much better. It is worth the money to hire an editor for a full-length article, since you do not want to discredit yourself by publishing written work that is less than perfect when you are trying to establish yourself as an expert.

Getting noticed by the media can take a bit longer, but just as with public speaking, you should start small and work your way up. Small-town newspapers are a great place to start, but remember you need to approach the editors with a story and not just offer your expertise to them. Tell the editors why their readers will be interested in what you have to say and how you can offer to help them.

One thing to remember: Unless your article or story appears on the front page of, say, the Washington Post, you will not have people beating down your door or your phone ringing off the hook. You are more likely to get noticed by people whom you already know — and a few you do not — when you get published for the first time. Use writing and publicity tactics to continue to add credibility to your business and yourself, as well as help with name and brand recognition.

Here are some tactics you can use when it comes to writing and publicity:

1. **Writing articles** — Articles are one of the greatest things that you can do. Not only can you publish them on the Web and then have people read it and call you, you can also use them as follow up for your mailing list or newsletter.

2. **Writing a column** — This is a bit harder, but once you get published enough in a magazine or online, you can start to pitch column ideas to publications that revolve around your industry. Then people who read your column will start to remember your name and keep your information handy when they need your services.

3. **Blogging** — For those who have the time, creating and keeping up a blog is a great way to get noticed and get your information out there. While it may take a while for the search spiders to rank your site up on the top, a constant stream of well-written material that contains the main keywords that pertain to your industry will help you gain credibility and visibility.

4. **Getting your quotes in the media** — A great way to get this to happen is to write or call media personnel when you see your industry being discussed in the news. They will remember your name and probably take your information so they can contact you in the future if they need more information.

5. **Having items published about you** — This is a great way to build name recognition and help get you and your business noticed. One great way to do this is to have press releases written and posted about new services, your business, or something special that you have done. These will then get read by people all over the Web and you will gain both higher Web traffic and phone calls as well.

6. **Gaining link swaps to your site** — Find other sites that offer items or services that go hand-in-hand with yours. Then contact the site administrator to discuss link swapping with them. It will help drive traffic both ways and helps you both out.

Strategy #5: Promotional Events

A great way to attract attention to yourself and your business is to hold promotional events, shows, or be a part of someone else's event. Participating in a trade show, cosponsoring an event, holding a fundraiser, or any other public event is a great way to increase your credibility and put you in front of potential clients, bringing a huge audience that you could not otherwise gain.

The downfall to this tactic is the money that is involved. To purchase a booth space, set up a display, and print and distribute literature and marketing materials to thousands of people can cost a lot of cash, so this is one of those tactics that you will really need to evaluate before you try it. Evaluate the cost of each solid lead that you expect to get from the event and see if you can beat that price by using a different tactic; this will help determine if you should spend the cash or not.

If you think you may do better with your own event, try to evaluate the cost that it would take to bring each person to your door and then evaluate how many good leads you expect from that event. You should always compare the pricing that you think it will cost you with the leads that you would realistically expect to gain from it before you commit to any type of promotional event. Remember that you will have to do months of advertising before the event, so make sure you calculate that cost in as well.

Here are some tactics you can use when it comes to promotional events:

1. **Trade shows** — Booths at trade shows can be expensive, but there are many different associations that will put on more affordable "table-top expos." Either one is great for collecting tons of leads, but not for closing deals.

2. **Demonstrations or workshops** — When you offer free demonstrations or workshops for your hottest prospects, then you can gain more than an offering of the same thing to the general public. These work like public speaking events, but you are in control of the guest list.

3. **Virtual events** — If you can offer a workshop or demonstration through the Web, it is a great way to gain exposure and leads. It is also a lot cheaper than many of the other types of promotional events, since you do not have to spend money on travel, literature, booth space, and so on. So if you are dying to host a promotional event, this may be the way to go in the beginning.

4. **Open houses** — Find any excuse to throw a party and then invite prospective clients or partners to your party. You will be surprised at the group that will show up.

Strategy #6: Advertising

Every business person has heard of advertising and knows the basics of what it is, what it does, and what it can do. But some business professionals find that advertising can be a waste of time since most advertising does not allow people to get to know and trust you. Just because advertising does not always get people to automatically trust in you and your business, it does not mean you should cut it completely out of your marketing strategies. In fact, advertising is a tool that most businesses will benefit from and will want to have working for them.

There are some types of service providers that will want to be sure to have advertising in print or Web page form, and probably have an ad in the Yellow Pages as well. For example, services that people may need in an emergency, such as a dentist or auto repair shop, will always gain new clients from Yellow Page ads. Other service providers that people do not use as often, such as heating and air conditioning or professional writers, can also benefit from Yellow Page ads, since most people search there first for local companies. And there are also service providers that people like to locate privately, such as a funeral home or a psychotherapist. All of these services, and more, can benefit from Yellow Page advertising, as your business is right there in its place with others that provide the same services you do. Of course, there are some service providers who will benefit more from direct mail advertising, flyers, and other forms of print advertising, as they offer date-dependent services like group work or seminars.

Before you set your mind on one form of advertising or another, you need to ask yourself the following question: "How do people usually find and select a service that I offer?" Write down your answer and use it as a guide when you are determining your advertising strategy. This will help to regulate your advertising budget as well, as you will not need to add in extra dollars to use a form of advertising that will not work. Remember that advertising can be costly, so you need to determine which types of advertising will work the best for your business and do not spend money where there is only a "maybe" chance that someone will respond.

Here are some tactics to use when it comes to advertising:

1. **Newspapers or magazines** — The classified ads in newspapers are great for specifically targeting potential clients. You can tailor the ad to appeal to those potential VIP clients and ask for an immediate response from the readers. Then make sure you track every response you get and it will tell you how well the ad worked.

2. **Display ads** — These are a bit more visible than direct response ads, but you will need a bigger budget for these to make them work. These types of display ads are normally placed in newspapers, magazines, or trade publications that are geared to your specific target audience.

3. **Yellow Page ads** — This can work for those services that people will look for in the Yellow Pages, such as an attorney or automotive shop. If you do not have a business that people will normally search out in the Yellow Pages, then do not waste the extra money on large page advertising here.

4. **Professional directories** — These will only gain you business from people who use these directories on a regular basis, but it does add to your business's credibility. If certain directories in your industry are an official source for information, then you want to make sure you are listed in it.

5. **Business Web site** — While a Web site itself is a multifaceted tool, it also is a marketing tactic. You can use a Web site in so many different ways, such as an online brochure, information avenue, and more.

6. **Pay-per-click advertising** — This means you pay for each click that people make onto your site. These can get costly, so make sure you put a daily maximum on your account so you do not rack up hundreds of dollars a day on these advertising clicks. This can be a great way to drive traffic to your site and help your rankings in the process.

7. **Banner ads** — These are online display ads that you have posted on Web sites and other areas of the Web, such as vendors' Web sites, that will help drive traffic to your site as well. Normally you will pay a fee for these ads on Web sites, but you can always speak to your vendors and friends and family about free placement.

8. **Direct mailings** — Mass mailings do not carry near the weight that personal letters do and can usually be a waste of money. So make sure you consider your target market and narrow down your mailings as much as possible to save on money.

9. **Flyer distribution** — While this is cheaper than giving out brochures, it can also be used to gain a larger interest in a target market. These normally work the best if you offer a special, limited-time discount or promotion.

10. **Radio or TV** — These can be quite costly, but they do have a great potential to drive people to your business. Make sure you have the budget to do these, and hire a professional to help you; do not try to do it yourself here.

11. **Bulk emails** — These are not recommended for any business. While many people try to use these to drive traffic to their sites, these usually annoy the end receiver.

In the End

Keep in mind that these are not the only tactics in the business world that are at your disposal. You should always keep your mind open to new marketing tactics and information as you come across them and you should never be afraid to try new ones that pop up. In the next chapter we will consider how to put your marketing tactics into a winning plan that will have clients flooding your office.

Chapter 19: Creating a Winning Plan

This chapter will examine the most important part of pulling in your VIP clients — creating a winning plan. This means you will be selecting the specific marketing tactics and steps that you will be using on a regular basis over the next month or more. Your plan will have all the specific actions that will start the flood of clients rolling in.

When it comes to creating a winning plan, there are several ingredients that need to be put in the right order to gain the results that you want. Choosing the right ingredients for your winning plan is usually just choosing a set of simple, effective tactics that your target market responds to, and then doing them on a regular basis. This is exactly where clients come from.

This chapter will examine all the steps that you need to take to create a winning plan from everything that you have learned so far in this book. You have learned how to weed out your VIP clients, market your business to those specific VIP clients in your target market, the beauty of referrals, marketing tactics, visibility strategies, and more. It is now time to put these things into action for you and your business.

However, there is a trick to this — all of the information you have learned will not do a bit of good for you or your business if you do not use them on a regular basis. This means you must use the plan you are about to create on a daily or weekly basis to get results, or all of the hard work that you put into creating this plan will amount to nothing.

When you focus all your marketing energy into one plan, and you actually implement this plan on a regular basis, you will find that results will come from the normal avenues as well as odd ones that you do not expect. For example, suppose you create your plan and start to use it on a regular basis, and one day the phone rings. It is a prospective client you spoke to a few months ago who did not seem too eager to work with you. Now she is in desperate need of your services and wants your earliest appointment. You never expected to hear from her, but somehow your marketing plan has reached her ears and she remembered talking with you all those months ago. When these unexpected clients come in, do not assume that it is by chance or accident that they find you. There is a relationship between the energy that you put into your marketing plan and the results that you will get.

The key to making your plan work it persistence. The more persistent you are with doing the daily or weekly tasks that you set out in your plan, the better the results will be. But do not worry about why persistence works in your plan, just take comfort in the fact that it works and you will see more clients roll through your doors.

Now that you know what this chapter will do for you, let us move on to the first step: choosing your tasks for your marketing plan.

Choosing Your Marketing Ingredients

There are a couple of different ways to choose the ingredients you want to put into your plan. One is to pick from the list that follows in this chapter, and the other way is to come up with your own unique ingredients. To design your own ingredients, you will need to know how often you do something and how much of it you do. This will not be an exact number or answer — it will be more of a guess. You need to determine how much of a certain activity you will need to do to get the results you want and figure out how much time you have to devote to that activity. The answer will be somewhere in between those two time frames. Keep in mind that no matter what activities, or ingredients, you choose for your marketing plan, you must keep doing them on a regular basis.

Now that you know how to pick your ingredients for your winning plan, you need to know how to pick them so that they will provide the results you want. You can do each different activity either daily, weekly, or several times each week. A "daily" action means you need to be diligent in doing it every day, or five days a week. A "weekly" activity means that you need to make sure you do it once a week, and those activities that you want to do several times a week, but not quite daily, should also be handled in the same way. The only main rule you will need to abide by to have your marketing plan work is that you will need to do each activity at least weekly to provide the regularity you need to get clients in your door like you want.

Now we will take a look at a list of normal marketing ingredients that you can pick from to use in your marketing plan:

GREAT DAILY INGREDIENTS	GREAT WEEKLY INGREDIENTS	OTHER INGREDIENTS
1 hour of cold calling	Send letters to 10 new people	Contact 2 potential partners
3 warm calls	1 hour researching leads	Have lunch with a colleague
Ask for a referral	Attend 1 networking event	Write 2 blogs
Give a referral	Make 1 new online contact	Comment on someone's blog
Call 3 prospects	Contact 3 former clients	Send an interesting item to a colleague
Call 3 referrals	Contact 2 groups about events	Speak in front of a group
Send an interesting item to a contact	1 hour promoting speaking events	Get your name in print
Add 5 to 10 new names to your contact system	Write 1 article or tip	Find new articles or tips to post to your Web site
Enter your contact activity into your contact system	Request a link on someone's Web site	Contact 1 media outlet about interviewing you
Send a personal letter to 3 prospects	Distribute 30 flyers	Update at least 1 page on your Web site
Follow up with 5 people	1 hour refining online advertising	Check out 1 new place to advertise
Make follow-up calls first thing in the morning	Attend a high-visibility event	Invite a prospect or referral to an event you are attending
Ask for 1 appointment with a prospect	Ask your networking contacts for 3 introductions	Have lunch or coffee with a prospect
Practice your telemarketing script	Get 1 new testimonial	2 hours researching your target market
Send 2 to 4 follow-up letters	Meet with 1 new referral	Follow up with 3 to 4 potential referral partners

GREAT DAILY INGREDIENTS	GREAT WEEKLY INGREDIENTS	OTHER INGREDIENTS
Plan your day out each morning	Make 2 queries about speaking or writing	Volunteer for a high-profile organization
Do all your "A-list" tasks first thing	Get 10 "no's"	Follow up with all your prospects within 7 days
Write in your journal	Reconnect with 3 former prospects	Attend 1 high-profile event
Organize your office	Speak at an influential event	Have lunch with a center of influence

**NOTE: Keep in mind that there are many other ingredients that you can add to your marketing plan; these are not the only ones.

Write Out Your Winning Plan

Now that you have a list you can go by to choose your ingredients for your marketing plan, you need to choose at least two daily, weekly, and other ingredients for your plan. You can always choose more, if you feel you will have the time to do them — but do not choose less than two from each category. When you have chosen your two ingredients from each category, write them down and keep them where you can see them every day until you these actions become second nature to you in your daily schedule.

Keep in mind that those daily actions are aimed at getting you clients right away. The weekly actions are those that are aimed at gaining great networking, partners, colleagues, and other prospects right away that can start helping send business your way. The other ingredients are a mix of the daily and weekly ingredients and all have their own special ways to help you get in clients, prospects, leads, and great contact information several times a week.

Make sure you keep your plan in a visible place — either on your desk or computer — where you know you will see it several times a day. The next chapter will consider how to set goals with your marketing plan and stay on track to keep those goals, gaining the client base that you desire.

Chapter 20: Setting Goals and Keeping Them

Setting a goal for your marketing plan, and your business, will help you to know if your marketing plan is working or if you need to change it up a bit. But how do you know if you are reaching your goals? You keep track of everything you do and you make sure you keep your goals in mind while you are going through your day-to-day routines. So, for the next month, you need to work steadily toward reaching your goals and also keep track of everything that you do. You will have to learn how to keep a steady pace instead of hitting the marketing full-speed the whole time or you will quickly get burned out.

To keep from getting burned out, you need to plan your week out ahead of time. This means you need to assign days where you work on your marketing plan and days when you just rest and take a break from it. Those days that you take a break from marketing are just as important as the marketing days themselves, as they give you time to recharge to hit it again the next marketing day. You can adjust the marketing and resting days as you would like. For example, if you work a normal five-day work week and you are off on Saturday and Sunday, then plan your marketing and rest days around that schedule. If you work a different schedule or you have a flexible schedule, then you can plan your work week however you feel best fits you.

On working days, you need to set out a specific time to complete those daily ingredients on your list. If you already have clients booked for those days, you work another job, or if you have other work to attend to that day, you need to be prepared to work before or after your normal work day, or do daily activities during lunch. You can experiment to find the best time to do these daily activities, to determine a routine to complete them all in the shortest amount of time. Do not let the work or activities that you already have scheduled be an excuse for not doing your daily activities that you have set out in your marketing plan. This will make your plan fail every time.

During your working days, take a few minutes at the beginning of each day to read through the marketing ingredients that you need to accomplish that day. This way, your business marketing will always be in your mind and you will know that it is something you need to complete that day. Do not make it the last thing you think about; make it the first. Make out a checklist of everything you need to accomplish that day when it comes to your marketing. This way, you can have a visual aid of what is done and what is not done.

At the end of each working day, take another few minutes to track everything that you did toward your marketing goals for that day and week. Take out your checklist and determine where your priorities need to be the next working day. If you find that you tried to do too much, you can adjust your working schedule to see where to cut back on daily activities or other activities. If you find you have ample time to complete all your marketing plan ingredients, then you may look at adding in a couple more to help gain more visibility and clients.

When it comes to your resting days, take that full day to rest and recharge. Do not try to squeeze in extra marketing or work.

Take the day off and do whatever helps you to relax. By allowing yourself the time to recharge and relax after a hard work week, you will feel better and be able to get back on track faster when the next work day rolls around.

Remember that the first week is a trial-and-error week. If you need to make adjustments to your marketing plan or schedule, this is the week to do it. At the end of the first week, evaluate how you feel you did with the marketing plan ingredients and how you feel you can improve your plan for the next week. Do not be afraid to change things if they are not working. But if you find you have a pretty good marketing plan and time to work with everything you want to do, give it a try for a month or more before you change any part of it.

The next few chapters will explore how to take care of your contacts from start to finish to help cultivate sales and appointments.

Chapter 21: Making Contacts and Appointments

Keeping a constant flow of contacts in the pipe will be something you will need to do as long as you are in business, which is why we will focus on this area a bit harder than others. One of the main reasons you are not bringing in the business you desire is because you do not have the contact base to back up the appointments that you want to set. Later on in your business life, you will be able to focus more of your energy on other aspects of your marketing and back off a bit on the contact pipeline, but you need to remember that keeping this pipeline full is something you will always have to worry about.

So, keeping that in mind, you will need to make sure you are willing to maintain your marketing strategies for a long period of time to gain the most contacts that you possibly can. When it comes to marketing, the more regular you are when it comes to different marketing ingredients, the better you will be. You cannot switch ingredients constantly and expect them to all work. The key is to find a few ingredients that you like, you are good at, and you can do on a regular basis and use them constantly. These ingredients will bring in more contacts that you can imagine. By doing these regularly, you will find they become a second nature and you will start to do them automatically.

Of course, you will find times that you wonder if the marketing ingredients you chose are working. This is natural and everyone goes through this, so do not worry when this fear creeps in your mind. It may even make you consider changing up your marketing plan to see if there is something else that will work better or faster. Do not let this sneak in and make you change up anything until you have given it all a fair shot to work. Be patient and allow your marketing ingredients to work for at least a month before you change anything. It is all right to change up some of your tactics, such as switching from cold calling to warm calling, but do not make any major changes to your plan yet.

When it comes to making contacts to fill up your pipeline, there are several ingredients that you need to have in place first. These are:

- A solid description of your services
- A well-written, short introduction
- Professional business cards
- Professional Web site

Each of these ingredients will help make your business more credible when contacts do a bit of research on you or when you are making face-to-face contact with people. You need to have all of these four ingredients in place before your pipeline will start to fill up and you need to make sure you keep all of these ingredients up to date.

Once you have these ingredients in place, you can start to concentrate on making contacts. We have already learned many different ways to make contacts, such as calling, mailings, events,

CHAPTER 21: MAKING CONTACTS AND APPOINTMENTS

and so on. Use the different marketing ingredients that you put into your plan to begin generating contacts for your business. Once you start to make contacts, you will find that appointments will come in, but maybe not as fast as you would like.

When you are making contacts with people, either in person, on the phone, through email, or any other form of marketing, you have these ingredients behind you and your business so people will automatically know what you are all about. They know you are a professional business and you offer professional services, so they will automatically trust you more than someone without these things.

When you are making contacts, you will find that most people will automatically say "no," whether they need your services or not. But if you find yourself contacting lots of people, but you are not getting any appointments or even making presentations to those contacts, then something is wrong.

First, make sure you are marketing to your target market and you offer a service that the target market needs. If you feel you have the wrong target market, then you need to research your market more. Next, look at your prices. Are they competitive with others in your field? Are your services priced lower or higher than others? By making sure your target market can afford your prices, you can eliminate that reason that you are not getting appointments or presentations.

Once you have looked at those two major items, then you can move on to other problem areas. Some common problem areas that most business owners run into are ones that they do not think about. We will go through some of the most common problems that business owners run into and what you can do to fix these problems if they happen to you.

1. **You are not using the right words when you talk to people.** This means when you talk to people, send them to your Web site, or call them on the phone, they do not understand what you can do to help them. So you need to clarify your Web site, and clarify your introduction statements to them so they know what you can offer them.

2. **Your telemarketing skills need to be improved.** This means you are either nervous or unprepared when you are calling contacts and therefore you are not able to engage people enough to get them interested in the conversation and interested in what you can do for them. You need to take the time to practice what you are going to say to contacts when you call them so you are prepared when they answer the phone and when they ask questions.

3. **You are not qualifying your prospects before you talk to them.** Perhaps the people you are contacting do not need your services, cannot afford your services, or they are not ready to use your services yet. So you need to take a look at your list before you make any more contacts from it. Make sure all the people on your list to contact are prequalified for your services.

4. **Your business is not as well-known as the competition or you have not been recommended by a friend.** This is a hard one to overcome. Most people will go with the business that is more well known or that a friend or family member has recommended to them before they head off to another professional that they may not know as well. The only way you can fix this problem is to continue your daily and weekly marketing tactics, as well as continuing to make your business visible and more credible.

5. **Your competition seems to have all of the market.** It can sometimes seem this way when you are starting a new business. No one wants to go with a new provider if they are already using someone else. This goes along with being well known or recommended; you have to keep hammering along with your marketing and visibility.

6. **You are not offering contacts what they think they need.** This means you are offering them what you think they need and not what they think they need. Make sure you research your target market before you start making contact calls or mailings so that you can write your marketing effectively to show potential clients that you have something they need.

7. **You are packaging your services in a way that they do not understand.** Maybe your services are bundled in a way that they do not need or understand. For example, they may want to pay a flat fee for services, but you charge by the hour. Do some market research on your competition and see how they charge their customers for the same services.

8. **You offer too many services.** This means there are so many options that your prospective clients are not sure what you really do. You need to size down the services you offer so it is easier for your potential clients to know what you can do to help them and make a choice as to which of your services will help them best.

If you are not getting appointments like you feel you should be, then go through each of these different items one by one and see where the problem may lie. Once you take a good look at why you are not getting appointments and you take the time to tweak what may be wrong, you will see a change in your appointment schedules.

In the next chapter, we will learn how to keep track of your contacts so you can maximize your marketing to them.

Chapter 22
Keeping Track of Your Contacts

Once your contacts start building up it will become harder to keep track of them. So you will need to find a good program and strategy to keep track of all the contacts that you make. There are many different ways that business owners find to keep a constant eye on their contact list so they can target their marketing better and can see where they need to improve their networking strategies and build their contacts. Here are a few of the ways you can keep track of your contacts to maximize your marketing:

1. **Find a good database program.** Many businesses use specific database software that is designed to help keep track of contacts, clients, vendors, and more. Most of these software programs will have special sections built in where you can print out mailing labels, send out direct mailings and letters, special offers, and more. These programs are specifically designed to help different types of businesses keep track of their clients, and you can seek out specific software that is designed for your type of services, such as medical services. If you are not sure where to start looking for a good database program, ask some of your colleagues to see what software they use.

2. **Keep paper files.** While this is more of an old-fashioned approach to keeping track of your clients, some business owners prefer to keep a hard copy of client information and lists. For businesses that only have a small client base or have a small contact and networking base, keeping hard copies of information on clients and contacts can be a great way to save on the costs of software. Keep files on each contact or client and constantly make sure the information is updated so you will always have the right person's name or address to mail information to.

3. **Keep contact information in a spreadsheet or other form of document on your office computer.** For those businesses that are more computer oriented, keeping client and contact information in a spreadsheet or another document can help save space that hard copies of information can take up. In this case, you need to create a document that you can easily change if contact or client information changes. This can also be a great way to save on the costs of software and files, and can work as well as any other option if your client and contact base is smaller.

These are just a few ways you can keep your contact and client information in an organized manner that will allow you to update them as needed. You should also have a system in place that is easily accessible to you, or any other office staff, in case you need the information quickly or if you want to have one of your employees send out letters, mailings, flyers, or other marketing information to contacts.

You should set up a system to ensure that, when you are at networking events or other events that will generate contact information for your business, you are able to enter this contact information into your system as soon as possible. This is an important part of keeping your list current, particularly if you are the type of person that might let things sit idle on your desk for weeks or months.

Once you perfect keeping your contacts in an organized manner and perfect how you can easily send them information or contact them, you will have a better way of following up with contacts after you initially speak to them.

GETTING CLIENTS AND KEEPING CLIENTS FOR YOUR SERVICE BUSINESS

Chapter 23: Following Up With Contacts After the Appointment

When it comes to following up with contacts after you make initial contact with them, most business owners will fall short of their mark. But doing a good job of following up with contacts is one of the easiest things that you can do in your marketing. You get every lead, referral, partner, contact, or other potential client that you have in your database, then call them, send them some materials, or in some way market your business to them to keep you fresh in their mind. Then, if you do not get an appointment or sale from them right away, you simply put them on the list for the mailing or follow-up contact next month and so on. Pretty easy, right? So if it is so easy to follow up with contacts, why do most business owners have such a problem doing it? Here are some of the most common reasons business owners fall short on their follow-up:

1. **Disorganization** — Business cards, phone numbers, scraps of paper with names on them, and other contact information can easily get scattered about your office on your desk if they are not put into a contact management system right away. This is why many business owners allow great contacts to slip through their hands.

2. **Priorities** — With something you have to do, it is always easier to do other things first that may be more fun to you, such as responding to incoming calls, answering emails and letters, and invoicing clients. But you must set aside a certain time each day to do your follow-ups with contacts to have a continually flowing line of clients coming into your office.

3. **Fear** — Some business owners think if they follow up with a contact they will be rejected, but if they sit back and allow the contact to come to them, they do not have to worry about that. So they avoid making their follow-up calls and emails to avoid being rejected. But this will only lose those great contacts that you make at all those networking conventions and events, and you can be letting great VIP clients slip away.

4. **Resistance** — Since follow-up is something you have to do, and may not be something that you want to do, it is easy to resist doing it. You assume you are great at what you do, so contacts should automatically come to you after you make contact with them once or after they see any of your marketing materials. But this attitude will only push clients from you as well, for without contacts and follow-ups, there are no new potential clients to bring in new business.

5. **Lack of the right tools** — This means you may not know what to say when you speak to a contact on the phone, or you may not have the right marketing materials to send to them when they request them. Either way, you need to make sure you are constantly prepared for anything that may come your way — either on the phone or in person or

through the mail. By being prepared to deal with follow-ups and contact questions, you will find more confidence and you will be able to pull more contacts in and make them clients.

Follow-Up Ingredients

We have seen a short list of some of the main problems that business owners have when it comes to following up. But what type of follow-up do you need to do and which will work the best for your business? There are several ingredients that go into following up that you can use, so we will go through some of the most common ones that work well for just about any type of business:

1. **Contact management system** — This type of follow-up ingredient is essential. Without the right information to contact people whom you feel are good potential clients, you cannot use any of the other ingredients that will pull in those clients who may still be on the fence about using your services.

2. **Brochures** — One of the first things you should have is a high-quality, full-color brochure that will give potential clients all the information they need about you and your business. This is a great thing to send out to potential clients and contacts, even if you do not think they are ready for your services. By sending out high-quality brochures for them to look through, you will educate them on yourself and your business and still give them the information they need to make an educated decision on whether you are the right service provider for them.

3. **Marketing kits** — A marketing kit is becoming more common than brochures. A marketing kit contains all

different types of information, such as a two-pocket 8.5 x 11 folder with a cutout for your business card, a fact sheet about your business or your field, articles either written by you or about you, testimonial letters from clients, case studies from successful projects, samples of your work, and more. Marketing kits can be a great advantage to potential clients and to you because they give contacts all the information that they need about you and your business.

4. **Short commercials** — This does not mean television commercials, it refers to that 30-second time frame that you have when a contact answers the phone or when their voice mail picks up. You only have about 30 seconds to capture their attention before they hang up or delete the voice mail, so you need to be prepared with the perfect speech to grab their attention and keep them so they will listen to you or your message and call you back. So make sure you have a good short commercial for yourself or your business and that you practice it until it becomes second nature.

5. **Model marketing letter** — This is a standard letter that you can easily personalize, such as with the contact's name, to fit any situation so you can mail out information and special offers easily. These model marketing letters should have all of your business information in them already and should be easy for anyone in your office to modify and send out quickly.

6. **In-house mailing lists** — This is the master contact list you keep in your office management system that holds all the names and information from contacts you have made while networking. This list should be readily accessible

to anyone in your office and always be up to date with the latest information. By keeping this list up to date and adding new contacts to it right away, you will be able to send out marketing information quickly and know it is going to the right place and the right people.

7. **Postcards or mailers** — This is a general mailer you can have done at any print shop. Choose a photo of your business or something that is relevant to what you do for the cover of the postcard or mailer and make sure you have your business information on the mailer as well. These should be already printed out, so they are not customizable, but you should be able to print out mailing labels from your in-house mailing list to send out postcards or mailers.

8. **Newsletters or e-zines** — In today's online world, the printed newsletter has almost become extinct. This does not mean you have to do away with it altogether though. It is always good to start off with a mix of online and offline newsletters that tell contacts, clients, partners, and other people about new happenings in your business, such as specials, new employees, and so on. Make sure you take the time to update your newsletter and constantly add new, helpful information for those getting the newsletter. By continuing to provide information that anyone can use, you will pull in those contacts who were not sure they needed you yet.

9. **Email autoresponders** — While these can sometimes fall into junk or bulk email boxes, the majority of the time they will go into the inbox. These email autoresponders are special emails that you write that are like mininewsletters and provide information about your business, specials,

and other information for contacts. These autoresponders should prompt people to check out your Web site, call you, or email you back for an appointment or a purchase. These can be useful if you have a well-written email that you send out. So if your writing skills are not the best, you may consider hiring a professional to do the work for you so you can simply send them out.

10. **Follow-up phone calls** — These are much different from cold calls, as you have already talked to the person at least once. You simply call to see how they are doing and follow up on any contact that you have already had with them. But, before you do, you need to have a good 30-second commercial ready to capture their attention and pull them into a conversation with you instead of just stumbling through a short call that they will forget shortly after.

There are many other forms of follow-up ingredients that you can also use; these are just the most common. Do not allow fear or procrastination to get in the way of your follow-ups, as follow-up activities are just as vital to pulling in clients as any of your other marketing that you will do for your business. If you neglect your follow-ups, then you will not see the business that you want coming through your door and you may make changes to your marketing strategy that will be disastrous to your business. Therefore, you have to make sure you are doing your follow-up work at least once a week, if not on a daily basis, so you can be sure you are getting the contacts' attention and building your appointment book.

Part Four

When Clients Start Flooding In

Chapter 24: Your First Clients
Chapter 25: Customer Service Basics
Chapter 26: Keeping Your Employees Motivated
Chapter 27: The Wonder of Referrals
Chapter 28: The Beauty of Advertising
Chapter 29: Specials and Discounts
Chapter 30: Cater to Your Client Base

Now that you have gone through all the set-up and marketing that will take your business to new heights, you will start to see clients coming through your doors. So what do you do when the clients start to flood in and you are at the point that you just cannot handle it all? Well, there are several different steps that you need to take to ensure that you can keep up with the clients coming in, while still staying on top of your marketing and advertising to continually pull in new clients and keep them in the pipeline so it does not dry up.

In this part of the book, we will talk about things you think you already know — such as customer service, referrals, and employees. No matter if you think you already know everything there is to know about any of these subjects, you still need to take the time to read and practice the strategies to keep those clients flooding in or you will find that the pipeline will dry up and your business will start to decline.

This part of the book contains some of the most important information that you could possibly need when it comes to actually dealing with clients and keeping them. Without this information and these strategies, you will lose clients to your competition and you may not even realize why. So, without further ado, we will get right into dealing with your first clients.

Chapter 24

Your First Clients

Whether you have been in business for a while or if you are just starting out, your first clients will be the most important group of clients that you have. These are the people who take the first chance on you and your business and then go out and tell all their friends, family, coworkers, and everyone else they know about you and your business. If you do a great job and they fall in love with your services, then their personal advertising for you will be some of the best that you can hope to get. But if you do not live up to their expectations, you do not do what they needed or wanted, or if you just do not treat them like the true gold that they are, they will also go out and tell everyone they know about how bad their experience was with you.

Think that word of mouth does not matter? Word of mouth is one of the most powerful forms of advertising that you can get. You cannot pay for it, you cannot buy it, you cannot find the right words to say on television to get it. You have to live out your promise to provide the best possible services and go above and beyond what clients expect of you to gain it.

Stop and think about how many times someone you knew told you about a great hairstylist, doctor, car dealership, or other business. They probably told you everything there was to know about that business, including the names of people that they dealt with, prices, services, how the offices looked, and more. You probably learned more about that business that you wanted to, without seeing an advertisement or information about that business anywhere else. Once someone you know and trust raves about a certain business, you are more likely to use them as well since you already know how you will be treated, and how the business is run.

Now think about the times when someone you knew told you about a business or person that they dealt with that was horrible. They probably went on and on about shoddy service, poor office conditions, high prices, terrible selections, and more. Their opinions of that business probably swayed your view of that business as well, and you will not want to do business with that business either.

It is for this reason that you have to treat those first clients like gold. No matter what kind of mood you are in, how the person is to you, or any other factors that can prompt you to treat someone in a less than perfect manner, you need to go above and beyond your normal services to treat them better than they think they should be treated. Once their first dealing with you is over, you can rest assured that they will be telling friends and family members about how their appointment with you went and if they liked you or not. You want to ensure they like you and you not only gain repeat business from them, but referrals as well. These are some of the best referrals that you can gain, from those first clients that you treat like gold.

Make sure you train your employees to treat these, and all, clients like golden nuggets. Remind them that without these clients, you will not be in business. Great customer service is the next chapter in this part of the book and goes hand-in-hand with how your clients, both new and old, are treated when they walk through your doors. So no matter how much you think you know about customer service, the next chapter is vital to a business and to keeping clients walking in your door and making appointments.

GETTING CLIENTS AND KEEPING CLIENTS FOR YOUR SERVICE BUSINESS

Chapter 25
Customer Service Basics

How many times have you been somewhere that you received horrible service? Probably several. At some point, everyone will run into a business that will provide terrible service; it is simply a fact of life. On the other hand, everyone will also run into a business that will provide service that is so great, they will continue to use that business for anything they need. In both cases, you probably told everyone you knew about either the horrible service or the spectacular service that you received and made sure everyone knew about your experience from start to finish.

Just about every business says they provide great service, and the vast majority fail to live up to this expectation. So why is it that they put it on all their advertising and marketing materials if they do not deliver? Because it looks good to new clients who may not have heard about them yet. To be different, you must remember that customer service is the backbone of your business and the very thing that will keep clients returning again and again — or point them to your competition's door.

While you are developing your business, you should strive to create a satisfying, and sometimes extraordinary, service experience for all your clients. When you can deliver the great service that you spoke about in your advertising and marketing, you will create trust with your clients and contacts that will strengthen your business and your abilities to gain new business.

Customer Service Systems

Every business needs to have a customer service system in place before even one client walks through the door. No business owner can afford to leave customer service up to chance or hope their employees will know how to provide great customer service if they are not trained. The best businesses will develop a customer service system that will operate on a preset schedule without any involvement from the owner or the boss, that will continually reach out to clients, both new and old, and help them to feel important to that business by communicating with them, providing them with the latest information, and just feeling remembered and involved with the business.

While a customer service system may sound like a lot of work, the benefits that your business will gain from it are so numerous that it is hard to even count them. Here are some of the main benefits that you will see when you have a great customer service system in place:

1. A happy client base that is easy to deal with no matter the circumstances

2. A wonderful word-of-mouth system that provides you with great referrals

3. High customer loyalty that prevents you from losing clients to the competition

4. A better tolerance for any type of price changes

CHAPTER 25: CUSTOMER SERVICE BASICS

To build a customer service system that will help your business grow and succeed, there are several different things that you need to look at. There are many things that will send business your way, but you need to know how to provide great service and get those great customer referrals that every business treasures. The way you do this is by knowing what your customers want. There are several ways to do this:

1. **Formal market research** — This means you need to find or purchase demographic data from special sources that will give you refined information about the people in your area who fall into your target market. This information will give you a better idea of what your target market earns, what their political views are, how high their education is, how many own their own homes, and so forth. With this type of data, you can get a better general picture of who your customers are and what they value.

2. **Informal market research** — This means you sit down with your clients in a relaxed situation (like offering to take them out to lunch or coffee) and take down some notes while you ask them a special set of questions. Some of the best questions to ask are:

    - What keeps you doing business with me?

    - What can I do to make your experience with me better?

    - Can you tell me areas where my business falls short?

    - What other services would you like to see me provide?

3. **Keeping in touch with customers** — This means you simply keep in regular touch with your clients, without any

bought information or any questions for them. This is the best way to constantly keep a finger on how your business is doing in your clients' eyes. A couple of great ways to keep tabs on how you are doing are with things like client surveys, feedback emails, and phone lines specifically set up for feedback.

Once you have put together a great client awareness system, you can log the data and analyze it to see where you can build up your customer service and where you are already doing a great job. The things you learn from these different areas will help you learn everything from how much money your clients make to how they like the wallpaper in your office. There are so many different things you can learn from these research methods that will help you build a business your clients love.

Customer Service Attitudes

When it comes to customer service, the difference between the good and the bad comes down to attitude. Creating a great customer service experience has to be part of your business, and not just a policy that you make your employees read when you hire them. You need to remember that customers are always in the process of updating how they see you and your business every time they walk through your door. Will their next interaction with you enhance their view of your business or lower it? There are some specific attitudes you should make sure to adopt when it comes to customer service for both you and your staff:

1. **You have to really love your clients.** You cannot fake liking people; it will show through eventually. You genuinely have to love your clients and treat them with care and

respect. If you do not, your clients will see it right away and you will start to lose them to your competition.

2. **You need to develop a culture that is centered on your clients.** The culture in your office determines how you and your staff interact with and treat your clients. Develop and implement a culture that will place the focus of your business on your clients' needs.

3. **Make sure you and your staff are focused on customer satisfaction.** This should be the basis behind your business and the overriding theme that you strive for each day. Do not fall into the old saying, "You cannot please everyone all the time." Instead, believe that your customer's satisfaction is your responsibility and the most important part of your business.

4. **The customer thinks they are always right.** This old saying has been debated for as long as it has been around, but it is still floating through the business community. This is because customers think they should always be right since they are paying for your services. Do not forget them, and remember that their version of what is going on is the only one that will matter in the end. If you approach your customer service from the standpoint that your business and employees are always right, then you will lose those clients.

5. **Underpromise but continually overdeliver.** This is easy to do, and makes all your customers happy. This means you will give them a set of expectations that are realistic and then overdeliver by providing the end result earlier than they expect. When you are able to manage your customers' expectations like this, you will find that your

referrals and how your clients perceive you will increase and those clients will continue to come back again and again.

6. **Customer service is everyone's job.** Make sure your employees know that their job is customer service too, no matter what department they are in. Do not throw around so many different customer service strategies that they soon become forgettable. Make sure everyone, from your janitor up to the president of your business, knows that customer service is the first and foremost part of their jobs, no matter if they deal with clients every day or not.

7. **Remember that people make mistakes.** Normally it is not the mistake that kills a client relationship, it is the cover-up or how the mistake is handled that does the damage. History is full of terrible cover-ups that have ruined people, so keep this in mind. Everyone makes mistakes — it is only human — and when they happen, be honest and open with your clients instead of trying to cover the mistake and cause a bigger mess.

8. **Try to anticipate.** Think about all the times you have been overjoyed by a company that gave you what you wanted before you even mentioned it. This is what anticipation is, thinking about what your clients want before they have to ask for it. While it is not ESP or a special sixth sense that you have to possess, it is merely common sense. Simply think about the things you would want from your services and try to provide them before your clients ask. By doing this, you will find that your customer loyalty will rise significantly.

Improve, Improve, Improve

No matter how long you stay in business, constantly look for ways that you can improve your customer service techniques. Remember that customer service never ends, so do not put a policy into place and then forget about it. You should always be learning and listening to your clients and continually giving them great experiences that they can brag about to everyone that they know.

To help ensure your customer service is always improving, you need to make a customer service manual that will list the procedures that you and your employees should use to deal with clients and give them the great experience that they deserve and want from your business. Here are some of the basic items that your customer service manual should include:

1. **Basic customer service policies** — Such as when refunds should be given, shipping options, key contact people for problems, when to refer a client to a supervisor, and so on. These are the main things your employees will need to know to provide great customer service on a continual basis.

2. **Customer complaint procedures** — These are the rules that will govern how employees handle customer complaints and problems, from forms and questions to ask to whom the forms need to go to when they are completed.

3. **Observations to make** — This should be a set of things that employees should look for when a customer is not happy so you can head off complaints and bad situations before they arise.

4. **Surveys** — Your employees should be able to hand these out to clients to get the feedback you need to continually improve your business and your customer service. Your employees should know the procedure for taking these and where to put them when they are returned.

5. **Key customer notes and preference** — This means you need a good list of any important things that deal with how your customers like to do business with you.

One of the most important things that goes along with improving your customer service techniques and your business is to have an employee meeting at least every six months to go over complaints and praise that you receive from your clients. This time can be used to look for causes of complaints and to help examine the ways that your business works with clients in the future to head off such complaints. During these meetings, you should set goals for your employees that should help your customer service improve, such as fewer overall complaints in each period, more referrals in each period, and more positive survey results in each period.

Recovering From a Customer Service Problem

At one time or another, every business will have unhappy clients. There is no way around this, so you need to expect it to happen. The question is, how will you handle it when it does happen? Do not panic; here is a list of effective processes that can turn a customer service disaster into a chance to shine in your client's eyes:

1. **Listen to and acknowledge the client's complaint.** You need to really be listening to the client, and not writing or doing something else while they talk. You need to

acknowledge how they feel, such as angry, frustrated, or disappointed. Then let them know you hear what they are saying and you understand why they feel that way. Make sure you validate their complaint by telling them you can understand why they are so upset, and let them know they are right when they tell you their problem.

2. **Apologize.** Admitting there is a problem and taking responsibility for it will go a long way with the client. Your apology has to be sincere, and not forced. Identify with the clients and let them know that you are very disappointed in the situation as well. Use phrases such as: "If I were in your shoes I would..." or "I certainly wouldn't want to be treated that way either..." Make sure you also positively reinforce them coming to you and discussing the problem.

3. **Let the client know that you can do better.** Tell them this mistake is not how you, or your staff, normally work and you will do everything you possibly can to ensure it does not happen again.

4. **Ask what you can do to make it right.** Just come out and ask the client what you can do to make the situation right with them. While this is a scary topic for most business owners, it is critical to recovering the situation and keeping the client. Make sure you are genuinely interested in what you can do to rectify the situation and also assure the client that you want to do whatever is necessary to resolve the situation as quickly as possible.

5. **Keep communication lines open.** Once you know what happened, what the problem is, and you have found a

solution that will make the client happy, keep in touch with the clients to let them know that you are working on fixing the problem. Keep a constant communication line with the clients until the problem is resolved.

6. **Thank them.** When the problem is finally resolved and over, send your customer a thank-you note for alerting them to the problem and helping you to fix it. Make sure you reassure them it will not happen again, and thank them for their business and the opportunity to keep their business.

The Secret to Getting Rich From Your Clients

Few business owners have ever managed to turn their customer service policies into a virtual gold mine. But for those who are able to do it, they find the one secret that not many know about — having a love affair with your clients. It sounds odd, does it not? But this is the true secret to getting rich with customer service.

Most business owners who are able to do this have a very small, select client base — those VIP clients we learned about earlier. These clients should be chosen for their appreciation of your personal brand and their affluence as well as their professional style. Do not just maintain a clientele to service; instead, maintain a community of professionals and surprise them with gifts and kind acts that will give your brand that 24-karat gold shine.

You should also extend this love affair into your employees. For example, if you have a receptionist, you need to make sure he or she is a highly polished professional who has a flair for making clients, both new and old, feel comfortable, and has a natural ability to smile and mingle with clients to help them relax. Other employees should also be polished professionals who are skilled at mingling with the clients and speaking with them in a pleasant manner to help everyone feel more comfortable.

One great way to ensure that your clients know they are your favorites is to use random gifts to treat them. These can be as simple as small gift certificates, lunch or coffee, or a fresh batch of cookies in the waiting room, or they can be as elaborate as a cruise, golf trips, or pro sports trips. It is all about your personal style and flair, as well as budget. By making your clients feel they are the most important ones you have, you will boost your client loyalty through the roof and you will never worry about losing your clients to a competitor.

In the next chapter, we will talk about how to keep your employees motivated to follow your business policies, as well as go above and beyond to help keep your client base flowing in your doors and not out of them.

Chapter 26

Keeping Your Employees Motivated

When it comes to your business, your clients, and customer service, your employees are the ingredient that keeps everything flowing together well. If your employees are not motivated or they do not like their jobs, it will show in your customer service and in your business as well. But if your employees love their jobs and are motivated to do the best that they possibly can for you, then your business will grow and your clients will always be happy. So how do you keep your employees motivated so your customer service will stay high and your clients will stay happy?

There are several main factors that go into keeping your employees motivated and happy in their positions. Some business owners do a great job of keeping their employees happy and others let this fall by the wayside, only to see the results in their business profits. To help you be one of the employers that has happy, motivated employees, you need to know the main factors that help to keep them that way. Here are the main factors that go into keeping your employees happy and motivated in their jobs:

1. **Environment** — Employees' environment at work is one of the main factors that can help to determine how happy they are in their job. If their environment is dirty,

loud, cold or hot, or in any other way uncomfortable for them, they will not be as happy or as motivated to do their jobs well. Employees must feel comfortable in their work space, no matter if they have a corner office or a cubicle, so you need to take the steps necessary to make the work environment comfortable for all. This can be hard, but there are several simple things you can do to ensure everyone is comfortable. Start with your office building. Is it too drafty or dirty? Are the work accommodations less than desirable when it comes to an office? If so, it may be time to look at moving your location. Sometimes the office environment can be fixed with a simple change in décor; wallpaper or lighting can help to lighten the mood of the office. If you notice your office interior needs some work, ask your employees what they think you can do to fix up the office. Just changing up the office environment can help tremendously with the mood in the office.

2. **Training** — When employees are trained well and have all the skills they need to do their jobs well, they are happier. They know what to do and how to use the tools they need. They know the company policies, and are able to work without much supervision. Make sure your employees have the right training from their first day on the job, and be sure you offer training updates throughout the year to help all of your employees stay on top of things in the office and in the business. Once you know your employees are trained the way you want them to be, and you are sure they know all your policies, you will be able to relax and do your job better since you know the rest of your business is in good hands. Therefore, by ensuring that your employees are completely trained, both you and they will enjoy their jobs more.

3. **Pay and compensation** — Of course, this probably goes without saying, right? A well-paid employee is a happy employee since he or she has no reason to seek out another, better-paying job. But a lot of employers do not think this way. They simply try to pay the least amount of money that they possibly can and get the highest qualified candidate for the position. These lower-paid employees will always have one eye on the classified ads in the area and you stand to lose them if they do not feel that they are compensated as they should be. This does not mean you have to offer every employee a six-figure income. What it means is you need to do some research in your area and field to see what other people in the same positions are making and offer a salary range in that area. This way, you are competing with other firms for the best employees and you know that you will be attracting the right candidates for the positions. You should also be able to offer raises on a normal basis, such as yearly or bi-yearly, and you should also have another form of compensation in place, such as bonuses or incentives. These help employees perform better to gain those extra perks that everyone loves.

These are the three main ingredients that go into keeping your employees happy and loyal to you and your business. You should not be satisfied to just make sure that these three ingredients are right, though. Always be on the lookout for how you can make employees feel more comfortable in their jobs and how you can reward them as much as possible for a job well done.

When you can keep great employees happy and loyal to you, they will provide better service to your clients, who in turn will refer their family and friends to you. Great, happy employees will not constantly be on the lookout for the next best thing in the classified ads, and you will know your business is being run by employees who are happy and well trained in their positions.

This ties in with our next chapter, "The Wonder of Referrals." In that chapter, we will see how you can increase your referrals with customer service and your great, happy employees.

Chapter 27: The Wonder of Referrals

Now that you know how to implement a great customer service policy and you know how to make sure your employees are happy in their jobs, you can start to focus on referrals from those happy clients that come through your doors. Clients who come in and receive great service from friendly people will automatically tell everyone they know about you and your business. But how do you coax good referrals out of those clients that will turn into other great clients? This chapter will help you see the wonder of referrals and show you how to gain more than you ever thought possible.

Most business owners overlook this virtual gold mine of VIP clients and allow them to slip through their fingers. Great referrals are inexpensive, and you do not have to spend a lot of effort to gain many, as long as you are following your customer service policies and you have happy, friendly employees to greet clients. If clients enjoy working with you, they will be eager to recommend you and your services to their friends, family members, business partners, and other people they know. In fact, you probably do not even know that the majority of your current clients have come to you by some form of word of mouth that you were not aware of. If you are not sure which clients you have that are actually referrals, then you probably do not have any type of system in place to benefit from the word-of-mouth referrals that you are getting in your door.

It is easy to increase your referrals and keep them increasing all the time. How many referrals do you think you get without any type of system right now? If you are not sure, just take a guess. Now take that number and quadruple it. This is the type of increase that you can see within the next month if you just follow some simple steps. Referral-generated clients are usually more loyal and better suited to your VIP views than any other clients that you can get.

Let us start with a quick look at your current referral status. By identifying a certain situation where you have gotten a client referred to you, you will start to recognize special patterns that can help you produce better referral results.

Recall the last time a good, quality referral came through your doors and ask yourself some basic questions about that referral, such as:

1. Where did the referral come from — from an old client or a newer one?

2. Why did your client refer them to you in the first place?

3. Did the referral come from someone who needed your services right away or someone who was shopping around?

4. Were you contacted by the referral or by your current client about the referral?

5. Did you talk to your current client beforehand about referring their friends and family to you?

6. How did you accept the referral?

7. How did you follow up with the referral and the client who referred them to you?

8. Is that referral still a client, or was it a one-time appointment?

While you were answering these questions, you probably started to notice some strengths that you currently have in generating referrals. And you have also probably noticed some of your weaknesses as well. Asking yourself these questions about your referrals will help you to see where you can increase referrals that you gain from clients. But this is not all that goes into gaining a flood of referrals.

Finding the Golden Opportunity

You probably do not realize it, but referral opportunities are all around you, and most of them slip past you constantly. It is not because you do not want the referrals, but because you do not recognize the opportunities when they are in front of you. To cure this and find the golden opportunities every day, start with picking out one day each week that you can focus on where and when you ask for referrals. Do not get nervous yet, this is just to heighten your awareness of all the golden opportunities that come at you every day.

Use a log to determine all the different opportunities that you had that day to ask for referrals from clients. When you are logging all the different opportunities, make sure you focus on all of the details of the encounter so you can overcome that fear of asking for a referral. By using a log of your dealings with potential referrals, you can see what will help you gain more referrals from great clients as well as what will not work.

Once you have a log filled up, study it and see where you could have gained referrals that one single day. By learning from your interactions with clients and where you missed golden opportunities, you assure yourself not to miss them a second time. You will be surprised, the next time a golden opportunity arises, that you find yourself asking for a referral from one of your best clients.

Starting Up the Referral Line

Once you see the golden opportunities that come your way every day and you learn how to grab them instead of letting them slip by, you will start to see all the great referrals that you can get without much work at all. Referrals are something every great business has many of, and something you will have to have in order to keep your business going strong. But knowing when those golden opportunities arise is only part of the equation.

There are several steps to starting up your referral line with clients and you need to become a pro at them before you will start to see that referral line widen and flood your doors. These are the steps you need to take to start up your referral line:

1. **Find your clients' benefits from referring people to you.** By keeping your current clients' benefits in mind when you speak with them about referring their friends and family to you, it will be easier to gain referrals from them. These benefits are the reasons that they keep coming back to you again and again, no matter if it is great customer service, or if they think you are the best in town. These are reasons they will refer people to you.

2. **Find out why others would refer people to you.** This means you need to know what all the emotional, social, and professional benefits are that go along with a client referring a friend to you.

3. **Figure out the type of referrals you want.** Keep in mind the ideal VIP client you seek with your target marketing, as well

as all that sorting through the non-VIP clients. These are the people for whom you will do your best work, and these are the types of clients you want to gain from VIP referrals.

4. **Consider where your clients meet those whom they will refer to you.** The goal with this step is to help your clients know who will benefit the most from your services and where their paths cross. You are helping them to gain a picture of that VIP client that you seek, and helping them match that with people in their lives who need your services and are VIP-client material.

5. **Teach your clients how to refer others to you.** You will be surprised at the number of your current clients who do not know how to refer people to you. You need to teach them how to bring up the subject and how to connect those that they know with you and your services. Being able to tell your clients exactly what you do will help you stand out from the competition in this area and will help connect you to the clients in a way that will let them know you are there to serve them.

6. **Ask for the referral.** This means just coming out and asking that VIP client for a referral from them. This is the part that makes most people nervous, but it does not have to. If you want to increase your referrals and your business with VIP clients, this is the part that you have to do. But the simplest part about this is that there are some great clues that will help you know when to ask for referrals from clients. Here are a few great opportunities that naturally can lead you into asking for a referral:

   - Your client thanks you for a great appointment.

- Your client asks you for other services you provide.

- Your client asks you to clarify a specific process or service that you provide.

- Your client tells you about a past problem you helped them fix.

- Your client mentions a friend or family member who is facing the same problems that brought them to your office.

- Your client mentions they are going to an industry conference that caters to people who you provide services for.

- You thank your clients for continuing to choose your services.

- You help to clarify their goals or help to make suggestions to work on them.

- You ask clients how they feel about your work.

- You compliment your client on their progress with you — this is one of the best ways that you can gain referrals from any client!

7. **Build up your referral connections.** This means you should offer to meet, consult, or advise anyone who is important to your VIP clients. Offering to help out a friend or family member of a VIP client will help them to trust you and know that you will take care of their friends when they come to you. This, in turn, will help build your referrals. Hand out cards or send out emails to clients that they can

pass on to friends, family, or business associates, or ask your clients to write down some people whom they feel would benefit from your services (make sure they give you a phone number). By asking for people your client feels would benefit from your services and then offering to contact them yourself, you take from them the burden of remembering and contacting potential referrals. This single step will help to increase your referrals by almost 50 percent.

8. **Follow up with clients who refer people to you as well as those who are referred to you.** By contacting new clients and those who referred them to you, you will find that you gain a more personal connection with them. When you call these new referrals to let them know what you have to offer them, you connect to them in a meaningful and helpful way that tells them you care about them and their situation, since you took the time to call them after hearing about their problem. Make sure you practice what you will say before you speak to them, so that you sound like the professional you are, and not like someone just fumbling through a phone call just to say that they tried.

Once you have these steps down, you will find that your referral business will pick up more than you ever thought it would. There are so many different golden opportunities that you are missing each day because you are not sure how to grab them when they arise. Now you know all the secret steps you need to take to cultivate those times and gain great referrals from them.

However, just knowing the steps and knowing when to ask for referrals is part of the equation. You need to be practicing what you will say when you are speaking to a client about a potential referral.

Here are some of the different factors you need to practice when it comes to asking for referrals:

1. Speak with a lot of expression and get excited about talking with that client. This will show them the passion you have for them and your business and communicate to them that you will offer these same great benefits to their friends and family members.

2. Smile at your client while you are talking with them.

3. Make eye contact with them, even if you are writing prescriptions or typing their information in your computer. Make an effort to make eye contact with them several times.

4. Be confident in talking with them about referring people to you.

5. Listen to your clients when they speak to you about other people they know, or when they speak to you in general.

These are the main steps you need to take to gain the most that you can from clients and potential referrals. By not taking these steps, you are letting valuable VIP clients slip through your fingers and into your competition's lap. Make sure you practice these steps and you try to implement them into your daily schedule. Once you are familiar and comfortable with these steps and how to ask for referrals from your VIP clients, you will find that it will start to come naturally to you and you will begin doing it without realizing it.

Chapter 28
The Beauty of Advertising

So you have gone through all the steps in this book so far — the visibility, the credibility, the trust factor — and you have made yourself an expert in your field. Clients are starting to come through your doors and you are gaining more VIP clients all the time. You have even become comfortable with asking for referrals from your VIP clients and those referrals are becoming VIP clients as well. It seems you can now sit back and let your referrals grow and your business boom, right?

Wrong. This is the time that you want to bump up your advertising and bring in some of your heavy hitters to advertise for you — your best VIP clients.

The beauty of advertising after you have done all the hard work is your advertising will go further and you will have even more credibility than you ever thought possible. To accomplish this, you need to pull in some of your best VIP clients and ask them for testimonials. It does not matter if you are filming a commercial for television or if you are working on your next newsletter; testimonials from actual clients who love you and your business go much further with normal people in your target market than you can imagine. You do not have to hire celebrities, and you do not have to spend millions of dollars on advertising if you have great testimonials that are true and from the heart.

Once you gain testimonials from VIP clients, you will notice that old contacts, new contacts, and even people from your target market that you have not spoken to yet will start to come through your doors for appointments with you. By knowing that other people use your services and that they absolutely love what you do for them and how you do it, people that never planned on using your services will want to know what the fuss is all about and will come to you for advice and appointments for their problems.

You need to grab these special new clients and make an impression on them to show them why those VIP clients love you so much. Once they see the value and the great services you provide to everyone, they will go out and tell everyone about your business and the services that you provide.

Once this process starts, you will find that your advertising dollars will go a lot further since people are already becoming familiar with your business and yourself. They will start to have an automatic trust in you and in your services.

In our next chapter, we will consider specials and discounts, which go hand-in-hand with referrals and with advertising. By using discounts and specials, you will pull in more clients than normal advertising alone, and you will have the opportunity to get in front of more potential VIP clients with less work.

Chapter 29: Specials and Discounts

Just about everyone out there has seen some type of special or discount that was offered in a form of advertisement. In fact, think about a time that you have clipped a coupon (which is a special or a discount on a product or service) or when you have answered an advertisement just because the special that they offered was such a great deal. Consider the times you used a different business than you normally do for services just because they offered a great discount or special that you could not pass up. After you tried out a new business or service provider, did you continue to use them, or did you go back to your normal service provider?

There are many different forms of specials and discounts that you can offer to both potential clients and to those who are referred to you. We will consider some of the different specials and discounts for both, and help you to determine which ones will benefit you more.

Specials and Discounts for Potential Clients

These are the specials and discounts you use in advertising and marketing to gain new clients from scratch from your target market.

They can be in the form of coupons, advertising specials, discounts for introductory services, free consultations, and so on. These types of specials and discounts are designed to get new clients and people through your doors and help to build your business. The problem with these types of specials and discounts is that you cannot control who gets them and who uses them, so you will have to screen your new clients and weed out the non-VIP clients once again.

But do not underestimate the number of new clients that you can gain from advertising specials. Discounts off services, free services, free gifts, and coupons can be enticing to those who need your services but are not sure about using a new service provider or for those who are using this type of service for the first time. By offering an incentive to come to you for their needs, you automatically gain a special place on their service provider's list, since they know you offer great services and you are willing to give them a break on their first visit to you.

Specials and Discounts for Referral Clients

These are specials and discounts that you offer especially to those who are referred to you and to those who make the referral. Normally, these specials and discounts are better than the ones you offer in your advertising, and they provide something for both your current client and for the referral, such as a special for the referral and a bonus for the current client. These can be a great way to gain more VIP clients who are already aware of your services, what you do, how good you are at what you do, and they automatically have trust in you since a friend or business associate has already spoken well about you. These are the best types of specials and discounts that you can offer because they generate VIP clients from the start.

CHAPTER 29: SPECIALS AND DISCOUNTS

When you are creating specials and discounts for referrals and current clients, you want to make sure you offer something unique or special to entice them to use the special or discount. Normally, service providers offer a free consultation, great discount on services, or other form of free item for those who are referred to them, and cash or a bonus for those current clients who refer people to you. This is a win-win situation for these clients, as both get something from the deal and both have incentive to refer people to you in the future.

You will need to make sure you cultivate these referral clients and your current clients when they send referrals to you. Thank them and follow up with both the referral and the client who referred them to you to acknowledge that you appreciate what they both have done for you and your business. By making sure your referrals and your clients know you appreciate them and what they do for you, you will gain more and more referrals from each side.

GETTING CLIENTS AND KEEPING CLIENTS FOR YOUR SERVICE BUSINESS

Chapter 30: Cater to Your Client Base

How many times have you heard of business owners who say they cater to a specific client base, but then just do the same general things for all their clients, no matter what target market they belong to? Just saying that you cater to a certain client base is not enough; you have to live the words that you speak. But what does catering to a client base mean? It means you put your energy into making a specific market more comfortable with your services than others; this is normally your target market or VIP clients. Then how do you cater to your client base? Well, this chapter presents how you can cater to your client base to ensure they know you care about their needs and you are a true professional they can stick with for a long time.

Catering to your client base involves more than just offering special discounts to certain clients. You have to take certain steps before you can cater to a client base. Let us start by looking at the steps you need to take to find the client base that you should cater to:

1. **Market research** — You have already learned how to do market research on your target market and narrow it down into VIP clients. You can use a bit of this same research for finding the client base that you should cater to, but you will need to refine it a bit more. You need to use the market

research you already have to find the clients that currently use your services to see which types of clients you want to cater to. Once you find this type of client, you will be able to find the client base that you should cater to.

2. **In-office research** — Do research on those VIP clients that you love working with. These should be part of the client base that you want to cater to and you should be able to see why you want more clients like these. Look through the clients you currently have and make a checklist of the things that keep them coming back to you and the things that make you love working with them. These checklists will help you know how to cater to a client base that holds all the VIP clients that you love to work with.

3. **Surveys** — In-office surveys can be a great way for you to find out what your clients love about your business and where they would like to see other services or items that they want. By using these surveys with your VIP clients, you will find ways you can cater to your client base without spending a lot of time or money. The clients who love working with you will be more than happy to do surveys for you and let you know what they love and do not love about you and your business.

4. **Suggestions** — You can also use suggestion boxes for both your VIP clients and your employees. Do not forget that your employees deal with clients as well, so they will also have some insight into what you can do to cater to your VIP client base as well.

Once you have all the research done, you can start to put together a vision of how you should be catering to your client base. For example, if a vast majority of your VIP clients wants to see a special service offered by you, look into offering it for them. If they make suggestions that are easy to do or changes that are easy to make in your business or office, do them. By catering to these VIP clients, they will in turn refer their friends, family, and business associates to you and let those people know you cater to what they want. It is a win-win situation once again; by catering to your VIP client base, you will gain more referrals and more business from those clients whom you already enjoy working with.

Part Five
Keeping Your Information Organized

Chapter 31: Software to Keep Track of It All
Chapter 32: Keep Your Business New

When it comes to your business, keeping it organized is a must. It does not matter if you have a paperless office or if you are a fan of the filing system; you have to keep your office and your information organized if you want to keep track of your business, clients, invoices, and employees. While there are so many different ways that you can keep you information organized, most business owners in today's business world are leaning more toward the paperless office and specialized software that helps them do everything with a few clicks instead of hours of paperwork.

In this part of the book, we will consider some of the software options that are available to business owners as well as how to keep your business new while still keeping it organized. By ensuring that your business is well organized, clients will see that you truly care about your business and that you are a professional they can trust.

There are many reasons that you want to keep your information in your office organized, and letting clients know that you are a professional is only one of them. You want to be able to stay on top of invoices, payments, sales, new services, marketing, advertising, and more. You should have your office organized so that you have your finger on the pulse of your business at all times. Your employees should also help to keep your business information organized so any of you can easily find information quickly.

When your information and office are organized, not only will clients be happier, but your employees will be happier as well. By having an organization system in place, your employees know exactly where things go and what to do with information when it comes in. They can then do their job in a more proficient manner and you will see a difference in how they work and how they feel in their positions.

PART FIVE: KEEPING YOUR INFORMATION ORGANIZED

If your office and information is not currently organized or if you do not have an organization system in place, now is the time to implement one so that both you and your employees can stay on top of things. There are many different ways that you can find organization systems to implement in your office, and one of the most popular ways is through software that helps to keep track of invoices, files, client information, and more. Of course, this is only one way. You can also use filing systems, databases, Rolodexes, and other forms of organization items in the office so that you can keep all of your business information organized and up to date at all times. By staying organized, you will find that your business will run smoother.

The first chapter in this part of the book will present some of the benefits of office software and how you can find the right one for your business.

Chapter 31: Software to Keep Track of It All

No matter what type of services you provide to your clients, keeping track of everything can get overwhelming for anyone. Sometimes a simple filing system will do the trick, and other times you need a large software program that is specific to your business or industry. So how do you go about finding the right way to keep track of everything dealing with your clients? Easy — you find a great software program that will allow you to do everything you need to without stacks of paperwork, long notes and invoices, and lost hours filing.

Since most businesses are now going paperless, software companies have to develop and price their software packages so just about any business can afford them. The competition in software development and sales can be cutthroat, which is great for business owners. There are thousands of different software packages out there on the market, and thousands of different things that you can do to find the perfect software package for your business. With the stiff competition, it is easy to find a software package that will do what you need and be easy on your budget.

When it comes to finding a software package that will help you keep track of it all and help you maintain your office well, there are several things that you need to consider. Here is a short list of some of the major items you should consider when you are looking at software packages for your business:

1. Are you going toward a paperless office? If so, does the software have a virtual filing system or large database?

2. Do you need an online invoice system?

3. Do you need automatic invoicing or customer call-back reminders?

4. Do you need software that is specific to your industry, such as medical or sales software?

5. Does the software offer a wide variety of options for you to choose from to customize the package for your business, or does it just offer a couple of different things?

6. Is the software priced within your budget?

7. Does the software company offer a free support line if you run into trouble with the software?

8. How easy is the software to use?

9. Can you learn to use it so you can train employees on the software easily?

10. Will the software run on your current office computers?

Of course, there will be other questions specific to your business and industry that you will need to consider when you start looking at software packages. You should make a checklist of the major items that are important to you when it comes to software, such as automatic invoicing, databases, virtual filing, and so on, so that you will know exactly what you need and what you can live without before you order a package.

You should also shop around to many of the different software companies. There are so many out on the market that you can find the perfect software for your business without spending a lot of money. Most software companies also offer free demos of their software packages, so you can try out the software and see how easy it is to use and how you will be able to adapt to it before you spend the money on it.

Once you find the right software for your business, make sure you take the time to educate your employees on the software. Also ensure that everyone is aware of any changes that will take place when the software is implemented. By keeping your employees in the loop when it comes to software changes, you will head off any opposition and problems that come along with changing software.

When new software is implemented in your office, make sure you inform clients of changes so you can head off potential problems with understanding bills or filing systems. Clients will appreciate knowing you are streamlining your office procedures to provide better services to them, so make sure you tell your clients this when you are discussing software changes in your offices.

In the next chapter, we will learn how to constantly keep your business "new" to clients so you do not become just the same-old, same-old to them.

274 GETTING CLIENTS AND KEEPING CLIENTS FOR YOUR SERVICE BUSINESS

Chapter 32

Keep Your Business New

In every business there comes a time when you seem to fall into a rut. You do the same things over and over again, and things become routine. Then that routine becomes how you do your job and how your business runs. Clients will start to notice this, and they will either fall into the routine as well, or fall out of it by looking for other service providers that are "newer" to them. So how do you keep from falling into the rut that can be the death of your business? You keep your business new.

This does not mean you have to constantly change your marketing strategy, your brand, or your business. It simply means you need to find new ways to keep your business and your services new to your employees and to your clients. There are different ways you can keep your business new to clients and to employees. We will start with how to keep your business new to your clients since they are the lifeblood of your business.

Keeping Your Business New for Your Clients

When it comes to your clients, you should always be ready to change things to keep them interested and coming back to you all the time.

You do not have to make major changes constantly; in fact, this can be a bad idea. You simply need to find new ways to make small changes in your office, your services, or your business that will show your clients you are on top of things and you want them to be happy with you and your services. You do not have to make these changes weekly or even monthly; normally just a couple a year will keep your business feeling new again to clients who see you on a regular basis.

Here are some easy ways you can change small things to keep your business new for your clients:

1. **Offer a special, limited-time incentive program for referrals.** This can be as simple as offering a $50 bonus to the client who brings in the most referrals to your office or as elaborate as offering them a cruise.

2. **Create a suggestion box and offer a reward or bonus to the person who makes the winning suggestion.** You run this like a contest and offer a special prize for the winning suggestion. The suggestions need to be about making changes to your office or services or business. You will be amazed at the number of suggestions you get from this type of contest.

3. **Change up the décor in your office once a year.** While this does not mean you have to completely redo every bit of your office and furniture, you can change up the paint, wallpaper, rearrange the waiting room furniture, or some other simple change that will create a new look.

4. **Offer coffee, water, candy, or other snacks in the waiting room if you do not already.** This is a great way to help clients relax and get ready for their appointment with you.

5. **Offer a new service to clients.** This can be as easy as offering a printout of your notes or important items from your appointment with them so they can review what you talked about or met about. Simple changes like this can help clients to feel more special and wanted and they will see you want to keep them in the know about their meetings with you.

These are just a few suggestions you can use to jump-start keeping your business new for your clients on a continual basis. You can use these suggestions to build new ways to keep your business fresh and attractive for your clients.

Keeping Your Business New for Your Employees

In the same way that you need to keep your business new for your clients, you also need to keep it new for your employees. While this does not mean complete policy changes each month, you can use the same simple principles that you use with keeping your business new for clients to help create new ways to do things for your employees. Most employees do not like big changes in their work environment or in their jobs, so keep this in mind while you are considering different changes to make. Small, simple changes, such as the layout of the office, new printers, new décor, a snack machine, or other easy-to-implement changes are often good enough to keep employees happy and feeling like you truly care about their well-being and how they feel at work. You can use a suggestion box for your employees to see what they would value the most as a change in the work environment, or to find other changes that you can easily make if you are not sure about what you should do.

No matter what changes you make, ensure that you are doing them to keep your employees happy. Do not make changes based on one employee or on yourself. You should always keep the well-being of all your employees in mind when you make a change or try to implement any new item. If you constantly make changes based on one employee or on yourself, other employees will feel their opinion does not matter and they will become dissatisfied with their jobs.

Success

In the end, you will find that simply following the suggestions, lists, and techniques in this book will help you increase your business tremendously. Even if you only follow a few of the different techniques I have shown you, you will see an increase in your business, even if it is not as significant as you would like. Just remember that the closer you follow the techniques in this book, the more your business will increase. You will find that some of the marketing, advertising, business strategies, and other things you have been doing have been keeping your business from expanding and in turn keeping your business stagnant.

So now that you have the tools to do it, go out and implement these changes and techniques in your business so you can enjoy the same success that your competition does and more!

Conclusion: In the End

Well, you made it through the whole process from start to finish. By now, you know your target market by heart, you are weeding out those non-VIP clients from your list, you have an awesome Web site and marketing materials, and you are networking intensely. The steps and tactics in this book can be challenging, and a bit scary, but are always powerful enough to help boost any business and gain those clients that business owners need and want. The rewards that come from following the steps outlined in this book will be the results that you have worked for, and will be well worth the time that it took you to get the information you needed to gain them. I hope that you will take a break and reward yourself for all the hard work that you have done throughout this book, because it was no small task to build up your business following this book.

At this point, you are an expert in your field, your VIP clients are loyal to you and only you, you know how to inspire those who work with you, and you know how to energize everyone in your business. You are gaining those VIP clients that you truly love to work with day by day, and they are referring their family and friends and other VIP clients to you constantly. You have your own personal brand that stands out from the competition and makes you truly unique, and it identifies you and your business to everyone you serve.

You are now starting to think like an expert business owner, instead of who you were when you started reading this book. You are still enhancing your knowledge of your industry and you are continuing to study the latest trends and information that relate to your business and your clients. You know how to develop an awesome, catchy sales process that instantly makes people like you and trust you, and you have started to implement that in every part of your business. You have learned how to develop the services and products that your VIP clients want the most from you, and you know how to have a sincere and successful appointment with your clients and contacts.

You have learned the ins and outs of networking, and by now, you probably belong to a couple (or more) of great groups in your area and your field that are helping to build your reputation and your business at the same time. You are making speeches, giving out information, and keeping yourself visible in all of these groups, and more of your business associates are starting to see the shining star that you really are.

While everything that you have learned from this book is extremely important to you and your business, it is even more important to keep in mind your underlying philosophy that keeps you and your business running. Never lose sight of why you do what you do, and do not lose sight of why you love to work with your VIP clients.

Now the question that you need to ask yourself is: What am I going to do with everything that I have learned from this book? Will I continue to use it and build my business and client base, or will I go back to my old ways in a week or two? Hopefully, you have learned enough to change how you look at your clients and your business so that you will not go back to the complacent ways that many business owners have toward both their clients and their business.

CONCLUSION: IN THE END

In the end, it is ultimately you who will make or break your business. This book simply gives you the information and tools that you need to become a great business person and to grow your business and contacts until you are overwhelmed with VIP clients. While this is the end of my journey with you, it does not means that it is the end of our work together. Whenever you need a boost or reminder of what you need to do, take another peek in the pages of this information-packed journey that you just took. While continuing on the journey we started together in this book, you will find that you will be challenging yourself more and evolving into one of the top business people in your field.

Thank you for taking the journey through building your business and your client base with me. I hope that you have enjoyed the information you read and that you have truly learned the best ways to go about gaining those VIP clients that you love to work with in your business. I hope that the strategies, tactics, principles, and general information that you have learned here will help you to become more successful than you ever imagined when you started your business.

Bibliography

1. Hayden, C. J. *Get Clients Now!* New York: American Management Association, 2007.

2. McNally, David. *Be Your Own Brand: A Breakthrough Formula for Standing Out From the Crowd.* San Francisco: Berrett-Koehler Publishers, 2002.

3. Montoya, Peter. *The Brand Called You: The Ultimate Brand-Building and Business Development Handbook to Transform Anyone Into an Indispensable Personal Brand.* New York: Personal Branding Press, 2003.

4. Port, Michael. *Book Yourself Solid: The Fastest, Easiest, and Most Reliable System for Getting More Clients Than You Can Handle Even if You Hate Marketing and Selling.* Hoboken, NJ: John Wiley & Sons, 2006.

5. Van Yoder, Steven. *Get Slightly Famous: Become a Celebrity in Your Field and Attract More Business With Less Effort.* Berkeley, CA: Bay Tree Publishing, 2007.

Author Dedication & Biography

"I would like to thank my grandparents, Charles and Georgianna Peay, and my husband, Dennis, who have always pushed me to do my best and encouraged me to continue chugging along, even when I was ready to quit."

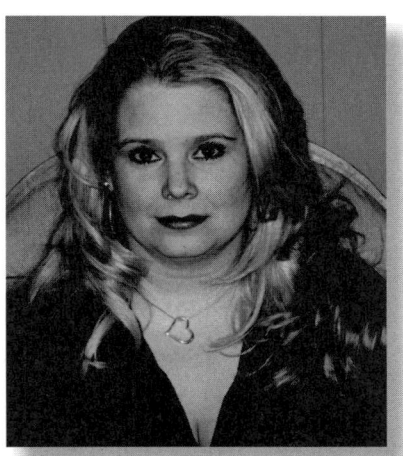

After running her own business for over a decade, M. D. Weems has learned the secrets that it takes to create a winning image for her business and the special ingredients needed to keep a successful business running smoothly. With all of her expertise in marketing and business, she has helped many clients find the winning combination to help their businesses succeed and grow. She has a proven track record that stands behind her work, letting all clients and readers know that she has the special skills they need to help them in the business world. She has written several books and hundreds of articles on business and marketing, which have helped to push her higher into the business world. On top of running her successful creative marketing consulting business, M. D. Weems also enjoys spending time with her husband and four children at their home in Oklahoma.

Index

A

Advertising 11, 25, 35, 36, 37, 43, 60, 85, 87, 88, 89, 93, 96, 98, 99, 101, 103, 114, 116, 122, 127, 151, 153, 163, 194, 195, 196, 197, 198, 204, 228, 229, 233, 234, 257, 258, 259, 260, 268, 278
Associate 14, 54, 141, 142, 146, 260

B

Benefits 17, 22, 30, 31, 32, 54, 73, 89, 108, 110, 114, 153, 171, 234, 252, 256, 269
Business 11, 12, 14, 15, 17-33, 35-57, 60-62, 64, 67, 69, 70-73, 75, 76, 80-93, 95-101, 103-108, 110, 111, 113-122, 126, 127, 129, 130, 133, 134, 135, 137-142, 144-149, 151-157, 159, 163-167, 169-175, 178, 179, 183-199, 201, 202, 205, 207, 208, 211-215, 217, 218, 221-226, 228-231, 233-243, 245-249, 252, 253, 255-265, 268, 269, 271, 272, 273, 275-281

C

Clients 11, 12, 14, 15, 17-35, 40, 41, 43-46, 48-51, 55, 56, 61, 62, 63, 69, 70, 72, 73, 75, 76, 81, 83, 84, 85, 87, 88, 89, 92-98, 103-106, 108-111, 113-115, 117-119, 121, 122, 126, 129, 133, 135, 139, 140, 144, 147-149, 163, 170-175, 178-180, 184, 187-189, 194-197, 199, 201-205, 208, 215, 217, 218, 222-224, 225, 226, 228-243, 245, 247, 249-265, 268, 271, 273, 275, 276, 277, 279, 280, 281
Company 18, 42, 43, 44, 51, 52, 54, 57, 67, 68, 71, 72, 73, 80, 84, 91, 100, 134, 151-153, 155, 165, 166, 186, 238, 246, 272

D

Developed 43
Direct 69, 81, 85, 88, 92-94, 96, 99, 100, 164, 172, 185, 186, 196, 197, 217

E

Elements 27, 52, 57, 107, 108, 130, 131

F

Family 21, 32, 45, 57, 65, 95, 120, 121, 130, 145, 146, 148, 149, 155, 159, 190, 198, 214, 229, 230, 247, 249, 250, 252, 254, 255, 256, 265, 279
Friends 20, 21, 32, 45, 57, 64, 70, 95, 96, 97, 121, 137, 138, 145, 148, 149, 170, 198, 229, 230, 247, 249, 250, 252, 254-256, 265, 279

G

Goal 24, 38, 80, 86, 97, 115, 130, 163, 207, 253

L

Learn 17, 20, 24, 25, 31, 36, 37, 71, 73, 82, 87, 88, 93, 95, 101, 104, 106, 111, 116, 117, 119, 139, 149, 155, 159, 166, 175, 181, 185, 191, 207, 216, 236, 252, 272, 273

M

Markets 17, 18, 24, 35, 99, 151, 153, 154
Money 11, 20, 27, 29, 31, 32, 35, 46, 50, 54, 65, 69, 71, 78, 81, 85, 89, 96, 97, 101, 105, 109, 114, 134, 141, 153, 170, 174, 192, 194, 195, 196, 197, 198, 236, 247, 264, 273

N

Networking 77, 97, 119, 125, 137, 138, 139, 146, 179, 188

O

Open 11, 48, 67, 92, 96, 100, 111, 117, 121, 122, 126, 145, 158, 175, 179, 183, 199, 238, 241
Opportunity 17, 29, 30, 31, 85, 97, 141, 242, 252, 258

P

Presentations 61, 77, 84, 191, 213
Promotions 11, 43, 72, 73, 81, 116, 152

Q

Questions 28, 40, 44, 45, 98, 103, 104, 109, 116, 162, 171, 214, 223, 235, 236, 239, 250, 251, 272

R

Referrals 21, 64, 75, 76, 83, 87, 90, 92, 93, 94-96, 97-99, 137, 144-149, 189, 201, 204, 228, 230, 234, 235, 237, 240, 248, 249, 250, 251, 252, 253, 254, 255, 256, 257, 258, 261, 265, 276

S

Services 17, 21, 23, 25-33, 36, 38, 41, 42, 44, 46, 53, 54, 67, 74, 78, 79, 85, 90-99, 106, 108, 109-111, 114-122, 131, 134, 137, 142, 147, 148, 151-153, 154, 171, 178, 180, 186-197, 202, 212, 213, 214, 215, 217, 223, 229, 230, 235, 237, 238, 249, 250, 253-255, 258-264, 268, 271, 273, 275, 276, 280
Statement 47, 110, 111, 126, 129, 130, 131

T

Target 17-19, 24-27, 35, 37, 42, 43, 44, 47, 49, 51, 56, 71, 75, 76, 78, 80-93, 96-98, 100, 104-119, 126, 130, 135, 140, 141, 151-157, 163-165, 170, 172, 178, 183, 188, 197, 198, 201, 204, 213, 215, 217, 235, 252, 257, 258, 259, 263, 279
Techniques 11, 12, 20, 37, 117, 239, 240, 278

U

Understand 15, 29, 30, 32, 33, 37, 62, 75, 82, 109, 162, 185, 214, 215, 241

V

Values 46
Vendors 125, 151
VIP 19-26, 35, 41, 75, 83-85, 88, 89, 92, 103, 115, 117, 122, 144, 175, 178, 180, 197, 201, 222, 242, 249, 250, 252, 253, 254, 256-260, 263-265, 279-281